PRAISE FOR
SEEING TO **LEAD**

A thought-provoking new look at educational leadership. Dr Jones gives specific examples of how leaders can grow and deepen their practice no matter their level of experience.

Dr. Nicole Semas-Schneeweis
Director of Special Education

Chris Jones exemplifies the concept of "teacher-centered leader" as he models it through *SEEing to Lead*, a true leadership gem. Exploding with ideas, stories, and most certainly inspiration, Chris shares his cycle of support, engagement, and empowerment as the foundation of his own leadership. Through wisdom and heart, he will take you on a journey, diving deep into each component, leaving one motivated to jump in. Whether leading students, colleagues, or both, Chris shares powerful ways to connect with, build relationships, and support those we serve as professionals and most importantly, human beings. From engaging staff to play critical roles in a shared vision to empowering them with countless opportunities to lead, Chris will motivate you to be the coach your staff needs to build a strong culture in your building together. This phenomenal principal will also supply evidence that all teachers are leaders, empowering all educators to make an impact at the same time offering unique ideas to recognize their awesome. Regardless of your title, *SEEing to Lead* is a must read and a book that holds tremendous power to impact your school and beyond.

Nili Bartley
District Digital Coach | Presenter | Author

Dr. Chris Jones delivers powerful strategies and an inspiring process that will help any leader create a positive culture in their school. A culture that not only stands for the greatness of their students but for their teachers as well.

Ed Gerety
Motivational Speaker | Author

SEEing to Lead

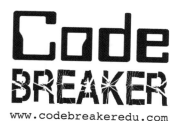

www.codebreakeredu.com

This book is dedicated to the other three members of what has come to be known as Team Jones:
Mary, Tommy, and Scotty.

Mary, my Bella, I can never thank you enough for the quiet support, constant presence, and ability to make me clarify my thinking. Whether supporting during the hard times or celebrating during the good times, you are always there. Your example of leadership in both the classroom and home inspires me to live by my word.

To my two boys who have often shared their dad without complaint, but instead a kind word and promise of more fun when given the chance.

Tommy, quiet and steady, you have shown me how a child, student or any adult can thrive in an environment that truly SEEs them. You are an example of those individuals with limitless, untapped ability waiting to be unlocked.

Scotty, full of energy and looking to make your own way, you have shown me that constraints should bend when they have aged past their usefulness. You embody the idea of owning what you believe to be right in the face of those who may disagree.

This book is for you, Team Jones. We are a team. You are my all and have all of me. Thank you. I could not love you more!

DR. CHRISTOPHER JONES

SEEING TO LEAD

SUPPORT. ENGAGE. EMPOWER.

ACKNOWLEDGEMENTS

Creating a true educational experience where learning, growth, leadership, and community takes center stage is a difficult, but completely attainable task. SEEing to Lead is about attaining that goal by employing a model that supports, engages, and empowers individuals to become leaders themselves.

The following people have been instrumental in the development of this framework and publication of this book:

Daniel Bauer, for his out of the box thinking, ruckus making, and ABCs of professional development.

BLBS Guiding Principals, for their perspectives, listening, questioning, pushing, celebrations, and accountability

Daphne McMenemy, for her talent, drive, vision, and perspective on teachers creating leaders in their classrooms.

Brain Aspinall, for his vision of continuous learning and willingness to offer me a chance based on the trust of a friend and short conversation.

Matthew Joseph, for his power of connecting people, desire to mine for the abilities in people rather than wait for them to appear, and "being unapologetically you."

The Code Breaker Team, for going before me and creating a well respected name to help spread this message. The ways their innovative, new ideas, and creative leadership has impacted me are numerous.

I would be remiss not to mention, although they are too long to list individually, all the leaders, teachers, students, staff members, and families that have in one way or another influenced my thinking. It is both because and for them that this framework was created.

My "just cause" of improving the educational experience for everyone involved by being purposeful, acting with integrity, and building character has lived within me for awhile. They have helped it come to life for others. As John Doerr said, "Ideas are easy, execution is everything." These people have all displayed the qualities of a leader who truly SEEs individuals and for that I am grateful.

TABLE OF CONTENTS

Acknowledgements... ix

Foreword.. 3

Introduction 7

The Struggle Leaders Face.. 13

The Destination is a Process (and that Process
is Circular).. 17

Support... 23

Engage.. 51

Empower... 73

Conclusion.. 107

About the Author... 115

FOREWORD

One of the biggest problems in education is tradition.

One of the biggest traditions that has existed too long in education is top-down leadership.

When top-down leadership exists, there is less room for the entire staff to have a voice.

And when staff lack a voice, authentic ownership of the school's vision will never happen.

That's the old way of doing school.

The new way offers something better.

By flipping the traditional model on its head, you create an opportunity for all to lead. The key is to really see and hear your staff.

And when everyone leads, you create an opportunity to do something remarkable.

And when remarkable things are happening in your school, the entire community is brought into the vision.

With everyone bought into the vision, you can accomplish anything you put your mind to.

Like having senior prom at Gillette Stadium in the midst of a global pandemic. That would be remarkable, right?

Or what about creating a Winter School that students and staff would want to participate in?

Or getting rid of midterms and finals.

Anything is possible when you see and hear the people you serve, whether that is the principal and their faculty or the classroom teacher and their students.

I first met Dr. Chris Jones ("Doc" as I like to call him) at a principal's conference in Philadelphia. I remember him having a great energy and having a dream that was much larger than his current reality.

In Philly, Doc told me, "I'm through with being a checklist administrator. I have a BIGGER dream for myself as a leader and I want to maximize the impact and value I create for my school community."

It was that conversation that started a years-long relationship and adventure with Doc. We would meet together with other school leaders to talk all things education and leadership in depth.

Here in our leadership incubator, leaders were free to experiment and dream big.

It was here where Doc had an insight that would change the trajectory of his school, his leadership, and his life.

What if a leader actually could S.E.E. their staff?

What if a leader used a framework where they could support, engage, and empower their staff? What might happen then?

The remarkable happens.

I'm glad this book is in your hands because I think you are the kind of educator that also wants to create the remarkable in your school.

The ideas presented in *SEEing to Lead* will help you do just that.

One of the things I admire most about Doc is that he finds plenty of opportunities to get into "good trouble." This is the ethos of what I call Ruckus Makers in education – those out of the box thinkers making positive change happen in schools.

I once asked Doc how he was able to create so many extraordinary results for his school.

In his words, "I think, why the heck not? I love to jump into the deep end of the swimming pool! There is absolutely zero chance I'm going to work anywhere where I can't be myself, because if I have to pretend, then it's not worth it."

If you often find yourself thinking "Why not?" while many of your colleagues mention "We can't"...this book is for you.

If you desire to create something remarkable, while your peers are comfortable and fine facilitating traditional education...this book is for you.

If you desire to not only be your true self, but are also committed to creating an environment where all leaders in your school can be themselves...this book is for you.

Keep making a ruckus,

Daniel Bauer

INTRODUCTION

My mission is to improve the educational experience for all by being purposeful, acting with integrity, and building character.

I arrived from a state far away and an environment that seemed even further when I landed where I would come to finish the rest of my K-12 educational experience. It ended up being a journey filled with more downs than ups. My educational journey has always been about taking the qualities of many teachers and coaches I am blessed to have been influenced by and passing what I have crafted from their internalization to you, the reader. This book is about my experience and how I have used it to become a better leader for those I serve. It's about the journey I've taken myself and that I wish to now take you on. I don't want you to take the same journey I have, rather I would have you take a journey that is filled with creating more positive educational experiences. For me it started with the idea of improving the educational experience for all those involved.

Elementary school was difficult for two reasons. First, I was an angry kid; the perfect storm of a father who had left both physically and emotionally. Being the young age I was, I had neither the skill nor the will to understand my anger and so I would lash out. That created issues in a school system not interested in why, but only what. Ultimately it caused undue stress on my mother, who was trying to deal with the new situation as well. Second, I didn't fit in with how students were supposed to learn. I was often bored, found it easy to pass exams without doing homework, and didn't build strong connections with most of my teachers. I have a clear memory from 42 years ago in my third grade classroom. My teacher moved my paper because she felt I was holding it at the wrong angle to write. But I didn't act out in class, so for the most part, I was left alone to sit and wonder when the day would be over. My learning was not supportive or engaging.

It was a night like many others and I found myself sitting at home listening to my mother tell me that I could do more and be more with tears welling up in her eyes. She just didn't understand why I wasn't a better student. That day had been especially long, ending with another after school conference with my teachers and mother. You know the kind. My middle school brain and I sat wondering the same why's they were. I had no answers. I only knew school wasn't my favorite place to be. It may have been the teacher who had me stand up in front of the class with four other boys while telling the rest of the class to get a good look at us because we would all be failures in life. It may have been the teacher who threw a ruler at me upon seeing that I had followed his instruction to write "I don't have anything to write" in my freewrite (every class started with 15 minutes of writing) journal. He missed. He also missed with the book he threw at me as I exited the classroom on my way to the office. That's when I really began to understand that I was empowered to do anything I wanted as long as it was exactly what I was told to do.

I had the same feelings of not being supported, engaged, or empowered – even though I didn't know what to call it yet – in high school. The difference was that I began to change my perception. I wish I could say it was a watershed moment where I suddenly accepted responsibility for not being engaged in my coursework, but it wasn't. I blamed my teachers, my situation, and anything else that enabled me to not look at the bigger picture. That bigger picture is where this book begins.

Any success I have found has resided in the second half of my just cause and as a result, I feel the need and am driven to help others be purposeful, act with integrity, and build their character. It took becoming a teacher myself after much cajoling from my friends and family as we walked the battlefields of Gettysburg and historical sites through Boston before I realized that I had been looking in the wrong direction my whole life up until that point. I shouldn't be blaming the teachers for not being supportive, engaging, or empowering if they weren't being given the space themselves to do so. Educators, like everyone else, need to feel as if they belong. They need to be supported, engaged, and empowered if they are going to pass that along to their students. I hadn't felt supported in elementary school, engaged or empowered in middle school, and any of the three in high school. So I spent most of my school career wanting it to be better and blaming teachers because it wasn't. It took a change in that perspective to finally understand that if teachers weren't supported, engaged, or empowered, they couldn't do the same for their students. I had now experienced first hand that they weren't. While those who took the extreme measures of moving my paper or throwing objects at me are not acting in such a way out of a lack of support or engagement, but instead an area of mean spiritedness; this more refers to those who strictly adhere to what has always been done. They do not change their practice by taking risks or moving to improve as the generations of students they see require. Instead, they continue to "go through the motions"and claim to still be teaching when in fact all they are doing is reciting facts easily searchable on Google. Like our students, sometimes all we need is permission to step outside that box, or opportunities to be empowered.

It was my first year as a full time teacher. I was completely prepped and actually a little excited as the students began entering the space we would call our classroom. I had planned what I considered to be an engaging activity to explain why the age of exploration played out in favor (in the area of amount of land) of some nations rather than others. They were going to act out the aspect of what country could get more land. I felt pretty good about it for two reasons: first, I thought the students would really be engaged and understand. Second, I was being observed and evaluated during this class. As the students arrived in this room filled with all kinds of excess furniture and other items, I began splitting them up by country. I wanted to make sure we had the whole class period and I could explain to the evaluator what I had done afterwards. She had yet to arrive. I gave each country a different color sticky note and explained that their objective was to put their sticky notes on as many (or what was perceived as the most valuable) items as possible in the time they were given. At the end of the activity, the team with either the most or most valuable amount of items would be deemed the winner. I started to get a little concerned because the students were fired up, and the last thing I wanted as a fairly new teacher was to have my evaluator walk into a room as my whole class was yelling and running around in what I was sure was going to look like mayhem. But my evaluator had still not shown up. I decided to let them go so I could take advantage of the excitement and inevitable trash talking and still get in debriefing the whole activity. The trick was that I let groups go in order of countries that had taken to exploring the new world. Amid cries of favoritism and "when do we get to go?", the students raced around with their teammates yelling where it was best to put their notes. Afterwards, with the kids slightly winded, we looked around and saw who had more. They began to understand the politics, negotiations, and treaties, which we would later cover in class. And in case you are still wondering, the evaluator never showed up for the lesson.

She did however show up the next day when I was giving an assessment. I explained what the assessment was and what the students had done the previous day. She took her notes and set up an appointment with me as she left. I still remember how my post-evaluation conference went and I'm sure you can guess. I was rated as performing poorly because the students should have had a more engaging experience. I took the opportunity to explain that I had planned an engaging lesson for when she was supposed to evaluate me. Her answer? "You should have changed your lesson for your evaluation." I informed her that doing so would have changed the sequence for the students and how they were learning the material. She explained to me that I had to decide if that was worth a poor evaluation. She went on to explain that what the students expect doesn't matter.

This serves as only one in a long line of examples where I came to realize that most of us do the best we can every day. Sometimes our best is impeded by skill or ability, but often it is impeded by mindset. We work to help students become successful but live in the reality of observations and evaluations that may not reward risk-taking, and instead look for them to fit a predetermined, quantitatively measurable mold. When we are not only freed up from a concern for our future, but empowered as well, amazing things happen for students in our care. For that, among many other reasons, it's a building leader's responsibility to support, engage, and empower classroom leaders so that they in turn may have the freedom, the confidence, and the excitement to support, engage, and empower their learners.

I want to acknowledge up front that this is not always an easy path to follow. The process of inclusion and collaboration in decision making is sometimes based on influences outside our control. As you read these pages I ask that you keep an open mind toward the possibilities that arise when you fully embrace the practices presented while understanding that there may be times you are required, based on your position alone, to use a combination, altered version, or very few of them. I also ask that you make those times as few as possible so that everyone may take part in the success that follows the authentic implementation of supporting, engaging, and empowering those you serve.

No matter the classroom or school, there are students sitting there needing support, needing to be engaged and empowered, and not having their needs met. I lived that scenario. I was that student sitting there waiting to be reached and tuning out because I wasn't. Now think of that teacher sitting there, acting out, or not coming along with the vision because they're not feeling supported, engaged, and empowered.

This book is a story about an effort to reach as many students as possible by leading in a way that leverages the power of those most important resources in our buildings, teachers. This book is about my experience and how I have used it to become a better leader for those I serve. It's about the journey I've taken myself and that I wish to now take you on. I don't want you to take the same journey I have, rather I would have you take a journey that is filled with creating more positive educational experiences. For me it started with the idea of improving the educational experience for all those involved.

THE
STRUGGLE LEADERS FACE

An old Cherokee is teaching his grandson about life. "A fight is going on inside me," he said to the boy.

"It is a terrible fight and it is between two wolves. One is evil – he is anger, envy, sorrow, regret, greed, arrogance, self-pity, guilt, resentment, inferiority, lies, false pride, superiority, and ego." He continued, "The other is good – he is joy, peace, love, hope, serenity, humility, kindness, benevolence, empathy, generosity, truth, compassion, and faith. The same fight is going on inside you – and inside every other person, too."

The grandson thought about it for a minute and then asked his grandfather, "Which wolf will win?"

The old Cherokee simply replied, "The one you feed."

This is the story that ran through my mind and brought me back from the brink of what could have been a disastrous meeting. Here I was, a new principal with all the ideas of how I was going to move education forward, even if it was in my own little area of the massive endeavor education has become, and this teacher who sat across from me was doing everything in her power to end them. These conversations happen everyday. Unfortunately, it is often taking place in the faculty lounge or the parking lot between colleagues. I was lucky enough to have it unfold face to face; in real time. She, throughout our conversation, pushed back on ideas about a positive culture, student recognition, increasing academic standards, and the need to stop gaining compliance through fear.

I steeled myself as I thought about the impossibility of a student being able to succeed if we focused more on ourselves than our students. I was ready for this argument. I felt as if I had been preparing for this moment for years.

Then, something happened to me as I took a breath that was meant to sustain the tirade I was about to release. The breath became less about preparing and more about cleansing and stillness.

That's when this story entered my mind. Granted, it wasn't the full story, but the gist was there and it was enough to make me continue with the awkward silence that had developed. That moment is when I was able to truly S.E.E. the teacher and realize I was going to make a conscious decision on what I was feeding.

This teacher's history had been filled with leaders who did not support her. Leaders who were not interested in engaging her in the profession as it made incredible and sometimes scary changes throughout the years. Most importantly, the leaders she had had for the past two decades had focused on control; letting her know that they were in charge and she was to comply. Now I sat before her, another administrator, once again trying to change her behavior. This teacher was not fighting me just to fight. She was facing fear of the unknown and a feeling of powerlessness to which she had been predisposed. How could I possibly expect her to transfer a completely different mindset to students in her classroom or the overall school itself if she had only experienced what I was witnessing. I took another breath, thought about her need to control and appear as if she knew the answer to any question I might ask, took another breath, and told her, "It's ok. I'm not sure I'm being clear enough. Let me support you in understanding what I mean and what it looks like so we both know what we need to do to be successful."

Her shoulders relaxed and her eyes grew softer as she looked at me and said, "Oh. Ok. What do you mean? I want to make sure I know what you are talking about." That moment was great. However, I'm here to be honest. Her and I still went back and forth quite a lot about acceptable practice, and that was ok because the moment I truly realized that for her to positively affect students, was the moment I realized she had to first be positively affected by me. That moment of clarity taught me two lasting lessons: First, I now take three to four deep, cleansing breaths (each one full, controlled, held, and from my diaphragm) before I have a difficult conversation or present at any event. Second, and most important is this:

You don't become a leader and then decide you need to support and recognize others more than yourself. It is the moment you realize it is about supporting and recognizing others that you become a leader.

It is not about being right. Rather, it is about creating an environment that assists others in their work to realize and act upon what they then come to understand is right for those they in turn serve.

This book is not meant to be about having all of the answers or proving that my approach is the only way to lead. It is about SEEing you, the reader. I am confident that the true path to increasing students' opportunities for success is about not focusing on the students but instead those who lead and serve them. While I have approached this book in a way that stays true to how I lead, it is framed in a way that supports you in finding where you fit in the area of student-focused and teacher-centered leadership, engages you in each of the steps towards a crystallized vision of what it means for you, and then empowers you to take the next steps. There are anecdotes, strategies, and reasons to explain the shift, but in the end it rests on you to make it happen.

I leave you with this thought: Have you honestly thought about which wolf you are feeding when it comes to those you lead? The wolf of no support, disengagement, and compliance or the wolf of support, engagement, and empowerment? It will always be a battle. We will not always successfully feed the positive, but understand; we will repeatedly be presented with the chance to decide.

THE DESTINATION IS A PROCESS (AND THAT PROCESS IS CIRCULAR)

Focusing on the topic of **S**upporting, **E**ngaging, and **E**mpowering those you lead sounds like an easy three-step process from the start. I use this image when I discuss this topic to highlight the various stages. It is such a powerful concept in such a simple image. We begin with support, move into engagement, then finally, we empower before beginning the cycle all over again. What is not shown in this graphic that is hinted at through its shape is the process that needs to take place from one stop to the next. It is an unbroken, continuous circle that has many blank spaces for all manner of people, skill levels, and stops

Image: Marcus Casey, (2019)

in between each destination. The emphasis needs to be on the process of how the wheel turns if we are going to make it all the way around.

Whenever I discuss the idea of SEEing those you lead with others, I explain why the graphic of a circle makes it impactful. In the end, this is not really about the circle of empowerment, but how success comes from applying the mindset that success in anything is not the destination. It is the process you use to get there. This process uses the visual of a circle for ease of understanding. This circle is key because it contains two important aspects by which many of us measure the success or failure in the recursive nature of our work. It must be complete and it must increase the speed of successful repetition (or revolutions of the circle) over time.

When I talk about completeness, I am talking about how important it is to not break the cycle. Often, as leaders we begin to support our teachers and students and work to get them engaged to the point they are ready to be empowered. We support this decision by giving them something that's a little stretch for their ability – like we should – and that's when the crucial moment comes. If they fail, we have the tendency to leave it at that with a drawn conclusion that they were not ready. The critical part of the circle comes right after the act of empowerment. As leaders, both building and classroom, we not only need to be there to catch them when they fail and let them know how to improve the next time, but also help them understand that failure is necessary as part of their overall success. Once individuals embrace this, they will be willing and able to learn from and move past failure. This in turn starts their circle over.

I was teaching a law class one day and realized that the students were struggling with being engaged in the material. Sure, I had sprinkled in a few activities to make it a little more hands on, but as we continued to move on, the class remained flat. So I came up with an idea. I thought that if I turned the curriculum to the often more exciting criminal law, I could hold a mock trial with the students serving as lawyers, witnesses, and the judge. I knew it would be risky, but wanted to try it. After a conversation with my principal at the time; hearing, "Sure, that's a great idea. I don't know how you are going to do it, but let me know if I can help." I was more encouraged than ever.

The next few weeks were a blur of selecting the case, assigning the roles, and securing a venue, and jury. Once the event arrived, I was super excited and nervous as the judge took her seat. The principal had been able to secure an actual courtroom for us! The jury was made up of parents (even my own mother) and the gallery was full of family members and other students. The night was an overall success as students argued their cases and listened to the judge's direction, but as to be expected there were some fumbling of terms, less than fully prepared witness testimonies, and nervous students. As I reflected on the evening, I also wondered what feedback I would receive.

My principal called me into her office the next day and told me she thought it was a very good project because the students were engaged in the learning process and it was an authentic assessment. I was all smiles as she then informed me she wanted to talk about how much time it took, material we covered, and the unpreparedness of some of the students. My heart sank as I waited for the bad news. Instead, I was greeted with a conversation about how to improve in a few areas for the next time I did that kind of project. I couldn't believe what I was hearing! This discussion encouraged me to not only bring in lawyers and a judge as guest speakers that actually ran workshops for the students, but to think about similar projects for other classes. For example, having the students research powerful families and famous artists during the Renaissance and then create paintings to better explain and understand the importance of symbolism during that time. But that is another story!

REFLECT

Think back to those moments that you failed at new things you tried.

1. Did you have a person that encouraged you to take that step?
2. Did they walk away after you failed or did they support you so you could try again?
3. How did their response affect your desire to take a leadership role again?
4. When interacting with others in the circle, how do you realize what wolf you are feeding?

ADDITIONAL STEP

If that person supported you, take the time to write them a thank you note. Their impact was greater than you realize. If you really want to take this a step further by challenging your perspective, write another thank you note. This time, write it to the person you supported in the face of a challenge. Thank them for giving you the opportunity to grow as a leader – a classroom leader or a building leader.

ONE LAST THING

Successfully starting the circle over is the first step in increasing the speed of revolutions of the circle. Each time you successfully help someone complete the circle, they will complete it quicker the next time. For example, someone who received the proper support that got them engaged until they became empowered completed one revolution. If you, as a leader, support them once they are empowered, they become engaged quicker and with less effort than the first time, which then leads to the desire to be empowered. When administrators support their teachers, they begin to see themselves as classroom leaders. They are empowered. Empowered classroom leaders foster these same traits in their classroom as they build empowered students. The cycle continues.

I was sitting in an interview for a principal position when this desire to be empowered became clear. The question was straightforward, but begged for a complicated answer. The interviewer asked, *"What made you decide you wanted to become a principal?"* I almost blurted out a philosophical answer that would show some grand design. Instead, and I don't know why, I stopped for a moment and looked at the 17 faces waiting for my reply. Then it hit me. I am not a complicated person and truly prefer everything as straightforward as possible. I decided to stay true to character and answer. *"You know when you are given some responsibility and the person above you makes a decision about a situation in which people are waiting for guidance?"* This was greeted with a few nods. I continued with, *"and when that person above you makes the call you say to yourself, that was a good decision. I agree with that."* A few smiles appeared. *"Well, have you ever been in that same position and afterwards thought to yourself, yeah, that's the decision I would've or maybe wouldn't have made?"* A few more people nodded and smiled. Especially at the part where I said I disagreed. I concluded with this. *"I now find myself in the position of saying, even aloud at times, I want to be the one making the decision."* I was met with a few blank stares as I smiled in the comfort of expressing my desire to be empowered. Even better and probably partially the cause of my smile were the smiles from two of the more stern individuals on the panel.

SELF-ASSESSMENT/REFLECTION

The fact is that everyone is always at some part of the circle. What differs is how fast they are moving and how much assistance they need. That's our job as leaders. As administrators, we must support our teachers, as teachers we must support our students. Find out where people are, what they need, and support them so they continue to excel. Our job as leaders is to serve. The faster the circle rotates, the more improvement and empowerment that's present for people to grow. The end result is a greater amount of overall success, less pushing and pulling by the leader, and more serving and offering opportunities.

1. Can you identify where those you lead are in the circle?
2. How fast are they moving?
3. What do you need to do to help them increase the rate at which they are moving around the circle?

KEY TAKEAWAY

Whenever we are looking to either improve ourselves as leaders or an organization as a whole, we need to realize that it starts by supporting, engaging and empowering others. Too many individuals believe they are leaders because of a title and as a result often point their fingers at others in the face of failure. It isn't long before they resort to tactics of blame and addressing areas that only serve as temporary fixes. To illustrate this point, whenever I speak to a group I have them all close their eyes and point their fingers at me. I encourage you to follow along and do this exercise as I explain it. I ask them to imagine something has gone wrong with a project or their team and they are blaming me. They can imagine any person they would usually blame, but for purposes of the exercise they need to pretend I am that person. After letting them point and think of why it's my fault for a minute or two, I tell them to freeze where they are, open their eyes and look at their hands. I then instruct them to turn their hand over and look at how many of their fingers they are actually pointing at themselves. So, down deep, who are they pointing at and who's really at fault?

Successful leaders understand their position is about serving others by helping them achieve beyond their original ideas of success. If you realize and act on the idea that individuals are forever at a different point in the

21

circle of support, engagement, and empowerment, rotating at a different speed, you will be able to grow those you lead; ultimately empowering them to step forward and elevate the entire organization. It is up to leaders to make sure those they serve continuously move through the stages around the circle with increasing speed. Doing this may sound (and at times is) somewhat difficult. So start small with a broad, individualized base of support for all. That will give you the ability to get anyone moving no matter their position on the circle. Let's look at how to do that next.

SUPPORT

*The cave you fear to enter
holds the treasure you seek.*
Joseph Campbell

While it's important to note that support isn't about always being kind or complimentary, we must keep four things in mind when we approach the topic of supporting teachers.

- First, no one, and I mean no one, ever gets up in the morning, goes through their routine, drives to work, gets out of the car with a big stretch and says: *"I want to suck at my job!"*
- Second, is a question that has plagued me for the longest time: Why don't we apply what we say about students to teachers? If they could do better they would.
- Third, is the fact that we, as building leaders, often prejudge a person's situation or motive before discovering the truth through a process of withholding judgment and investigating.
- Fourth, whenever you are meeting with a teacher to correct a misstep or improve a practice, never, and I mean never say, "What I'm telling you is what's best for kids." It automatically implies that teachers are not doing what they believe to be best for kids. We know that is not true.

After months or even possibly years of repeated trips to both the pediatrician and emergency department, I found myself sitting in the hospital once again. This time we had tried to just stay with the pediatrician's subscribed steroid and a humidifier in my son's room, but he had gotten no better. As I waited for our turn, I was texting back and forth with my wife who was home with our other son. Our statements were the same. We both believed we had an excellent pediatrician who was doing all the right things to treat the symptoms, but that was just it. They would keep returning. Why couldn't we treat the cause? After watching the doctors put my scared 6 year old in what looked like a medieval contraption to make sure they could get good x-rays of his chest and relaying the image to my wife when I returned home, we decided to make sure we got serious about finding the cause. Our next stop was to set an appointment with a pediatric pulmonologist.

The amount of paperwork was daunting. We needed to complete, recover, and write about every aspect of my son's medical history from birth. Actually, before birth because of questions pertaining to the pregnancy. We were both honestly a little frustrated at having to go through the paperwork and getting an appointment. Why couldn't we just get to the solution for our son? So there we were, sitting in the doctor's office with both boys, waiting to be seen. Like most doctors' appointments, he was a little late. Our anxiety grew as both boys were getting restless. What followed after that still astonishes me to this day and serves as a model for the type of leader I want to be when it comes to supporting those I serve. This doctor spent two hours examining our son and going over his complete history with us. The result from that visit was a series of tests at Boston Children's Hospital. Realizing we were both in education (because he actually read the paperwork and studied our case), he made sure we were scheduled for the very next week because it was over vacation. In fact, he scheduled it so we wouldn't get stuck in traffic as well. We both left that evening feeling a little nervous about the upcoming tests, but as if we were being supported in a manner that would work for not just us, but our son. That nervousness returned at the hospital.

We spent the day watching our son go through what seemed to be unending tests. He was moved from one waiting area to the other, put into multiple air chambers, and had his blood tested. Once it was over we returned home and scheduled our next visit for the results. This appointment was not as long. We sat in the office as the doctor gave us the news that we thought we had been waiting for. He did so by ruling out some of the major health concerns first. Then he confidently proclaimed what he thought was the root cause, why he believed it, and how we could go about fixing it without any more heavy medications or trips to the hospital. This doctor listened to us, respected our desire to find the cause so that we could support our son in the long term, helped us identify it, and as a result, my son's lungs have not had an issue since.

The first and arguably most important aspect of supporting anyone, especially teachers, is the ability to build an understanding between the two people.

If you are going to successfully support someone, you have to understand not just where they need support, but also why.

Completing the former while ignoring the latter does nothing but mask the true problems. In essence, it treats the symptoms rather than creating a cure.

For example, one end of the spectrum is that a teacher needs support, but doesn't realize their level of need. They are trying (refer to number two above), but cannot discern where the issue is or how to start addressing the problem. At the other end is the teacher who is comfortable with how they are performing. It is good enough, they are comfortable, and as a result see no need to change, much less be supported through such a move.

Determining where a teacher fits along this spectrum, what they need to continue improving, and why they are at that point is often the problem. It requires trust, honesty, and an openness to discovering more; by both the person needing and the one giving the support.

This is one of the pieces that make successfully supporting people so inspiring and difficult at the same time. Once a person takes on the role of helping another person, they have to realize that any assistance they offer must come from the inside out.

Successful support or even leadership is not about exerting force or a solution from the outside, rather it is the acknowledgement of an opportunity to help

someone understand and then act on their ability to change for the better.

Once you have fostered that realization, people can become engaged and ultimately empowered to continually grow. Authentic growth occurs when a person makes up their mind to take action. As administrators helping teachers, it must be our calling to offer that safety of support so doubt, discouragement, negativity, and the idea of accepting status quo are unable to take root.

As administrators it is our duty to help teachers grow and better their practice. It is always easy to move to the default that those we serve are purposely making mistakes because they don't care enough about the current situation. This becomes even more painfully evident when it appears they don't care about what we want them to care about which in essence is what we care about. In other words, our frustration with the idea that the agenda we want isn't being fulfilled. Let's take a moment and complete an activity that Brené Brown outlined in her book, *Rising Strong.*[1]

EXERCISE

Take out a piece of paper and write down the name of someone who fills you with frustration, resentment, and anger. Close your eyes for a moment and really picture some of the things this person has done to make the top of your list. Live with that feeling of frustration for a moment. Make it real for yourself as if they were doing the same act again.

Now stop and take a couple of breaths to clear your mind. Ask yourself, what if that person is doing the best they can? What emotion did that bring to the surface? How did you answer the question? Your answer may take some reflection. Brené Brown's research proposes that, if honest, you might be surprised because "as crazy as it sounds, many of us will choose to stay in the resentment, disappointment, and frustration that come with believing people aren't trying rather than face a difficult conversation about real deficits."[2] It's easy to live in the jaded, unhelpful perception often taken in education and use the saying, "Then maybe they just need to go somewhere else. This isn't the job for them."

Think about that assertion for a moment. How many conversations about performance deficits are you not having because it is uncomfortable for you? How uncomfortable do you think it is for the teacher who knows (because they do know) they are performing in an unsatisfactory way, but instead of receiving real support are just being told how they are unsatisfactory? Or worse, they are ignored, allowing an administrator to avoid the frustration they feel whenever they have to deal with that person. The real question then becomes about how we, as building leaders, adjust our frame of reference and step into those difficult conversations to enact improvement rather than an accepted mediocrity. In effect, how we as leaders go into that cave we fear that holds the treasure we seek, as Joseph Cambell best put it.

Support is a tricky endeavor. There is often confusion about the process, meaning, and outcome of support. The support those in our buildings require if they are to find greater success is often as different as the individuals themselves. They have both personal and professional aspects that affect their performance. As a result, it must be individualized. One other aspect of support is very clear. It cannot be a difficult conversation that appears suddenly out of the blue or a passing inquiry about a person's struggles that resembles the pat answer to "how are you today?" Doing so creates an atmosphere that feels contrived or even worse as if the leader has already made up their mind about a person's ability. The first step to supporting teachers is realizing that it isn't about having low expectations for them as professionals.

Teachers that need support are going to struggle, but over-protecting, making excuses, or doing too much for them will not help, but instead hurt or slow down their growth as professionals. Real support is about holding high standards and then making sure teachers have the feedback and tools they need to continue to improve professionally while feeling accepted personally. Do this right and your teachers will pay you back in the best way possible; engagement and a desire to continually improve at the ultimate benefit of the students. So how does this happen? If leaders want to authentically support teachers, we need to engage in a consistent loop of observing, feedback, listening, and providing what they need. Executing these four steps can be a difficult task with many obstacles because they are so tightly tied to our personal perspective, actions, and context.

Like any journey into a cave, you have to be prepared for difficulties and failures along the way. Consider outfitting a person to take a trip. We want that person to have a great time and overall successful experience. So do we give them what we would need for that same result or discover what they as an individual will need and provide them with that? This is what leaders need to do if they are to successfully support teachers. It doesn't sound as difficult as it is, but leaders must attempt to support teachers not from where the leader wants them to be, but instead from an objective assessment of who and what they actually are. **Most importantly**, whenever a leader attempts to support someone, a relationship is required. It is the make-up and strength of that relationship that will determine success or failure. Support, while difficult, can be incredibly rewarding as growth begins to occur, but also very frustrating if it continues to fail due to a flawed process. That process of observing, feedback, listening, and providing what teachers need must take place in three areas: building trust, coaching, and creating a map.

THE TRUTH ABOUT BUILDING TRUST

You have all heard the phrase about trust taking a lifetime to build and only a moment to lose. That does have some truth to it, but only insofar as the time ratio. Trust does take time to build so focusing on those small, consistent actions is important. However, this is another area in which leaders must adjust their perspective if they are going to find success. If the most effective way to support someone is to find out what they really need, you must be able to have them open up and communicate with you. Think about the following: when we don't have trust built up or feel as if we can't trust, it leads us to talk **about** people rather than **to** them. Remember, trust is the loudest voice in the room when a person asks themselves, "is this person really trying to help me?" Whether it's positive or negative depends on how consistently that process has been followed.

EXERCISE

Think about a person you don't trust who can evaluate you. Reflect back on the last conversation you had with them. Remember what it was like as they offered you support moving forward. This is often (if being done thoroughly) completed by questioning to have you share where you need to improve. Get a detailed picture in your mind about the difference between what you told them and what you held back for fear of not trusting what they would do with the information. Ask yourself how valuable that difference in information is for supporting your growth. Here is the hard, but honest question. How many times are you as a leader missing the opportunity to authentically support someone because you are missing that piece of information due to a lack of trust?

ACTION STEPS

1. BUILD A RELATIONSHIP: It is never too late to begin deepening a relationship with those you lead—be it students, or teachers. Having a relationship with them helps facilitate honest and authentic feedback between the two of you. Focus on who individuals are as people rather than their titles. I use surveys that ask questions about favorite music, snacks, and bucket lists to begin this process. Adding a personal touch that on the surface has nothing to do with the work they're doing builds connections between individuals. I also work very hard to empathize with those I serve. In short, I put myself in their shoes and ask what I would want for support given the different perspectives or needs I may be currently experiencing.

2. LISTEN: Remember those surveys about their likes, needs, and aspirations? I also have a weekly check-in form that I use. I use all of that information to facilitate conversations about their lives, personal situations, and struggles. This allows me to understand and support someone who has an issue with daycare without making it a big deal. There are teachers who are a little less prepared because they are taking care of an ailing parent or experiencing problems at home as opposed to just being unprepared or disorganized. Each one needs a different level or type of support. Leaders who do not listen are unable to successfully build trust and therefore support individuals. Even if teachers do not immediately share the deeper information with you, there is still the opportunity to build trust by consistently asking about topics other than work. People inherently like to talk about themselves and their lives. All you have to do is listen long enough to let them. Then act on what they tell you.

3. CONDUCT FREQUENT AND OBJECTIVE OBSERVATIONS: Traditionally, evaluations are when trust is most vulnerable. After all, the person is being judged in a manner that makes it feel as if it is about them as a person rather than the act in which they are engaging.

Leaders can combat this personalization by getting into classrooms as often as possible and providing informal feedback as a way to form a foundation of trust. It is important to use a process that follows a spectrum when doing this. If you are starting a new relationship, just observe for a while without making a judgement. Ask clarifying questions about what you saw. This shows interest in you learning more before you pass judgement. In essence, it places value on the teacher as a professional. I have learned so much just by asking questions about what I am observing. As some time progresses, start giving feedback in a manner that is positive and asks questions. A personal favorite tool of mine is Voxer.[3] Teachers will then see you more as an objective voice and be open to constructive feedback and suggestions based on the rapport you have built.

The most important thing to realize through all of these action steps to build both personal and professional trust is that consistency is key. Interact with your teachers often, continually listen to what is occurring in their lives, and frequently observe them in their practice. And let them do the same for you. How can we ever expect our teachers to trust us if we don't do the same in return? We will talk much more about the reciprocal nature of this relationship when we address engagement and empowerment.

BE A COACH, NOT A MENTOR

If you are doing your job according to requirements and "best practices" your teachers already have a mentor. That is not your role. Yes, you are trying to build a deeper level of trust, but in the end you are still the evaluator. As a result, if your teachers are going to be successful, they need that friendship type relationship with a person who will hear their concerns, insecurities, failures, and personal victories. These two roles are close to the same, but the coach (you) needs to get a specific performance or result from the player (teacher). As a result, the relationship has to be and is different.

It was early and I had already spent two hours assembling, loading onto a bus, slathering on government issued DEET, driving around Paris Island, and following the intake procedure for recruits; screaming and all. As I stood watching some recruits performing physical training while waiting my turn on one of the obstacles on the Confidence Course, my Drill Instructor (DI) was explaining some of the process and meaning behind Marine Basic Training. He informed me that their training is designed to achieve a very specific performance outcome and as a result, they have to build their recruits up, but still have a relationship of expectations with them. The DI then went on to explain that their role isn't like in the movies.

Yes, it is a lot of yelling and barking orders, but as the training moves forward, the DIs begin to gradually release some of that control until the end when they work side by side with the recruits. They continue to correct and adjust, but that relationship is there. When I asked for clarification, he was happy to explain that there is a very real chance that something may happen to the leader in the field and that means they need to train thinkers that can take over "in the event someone goes down or a problem arises."

I realize that teaching is not the Marines, but it is a performance-based practice. As a result, there will be successes and failures.

The role of a leader has to be supportive by focusing on a teacher's strengths as a place to build on as difficulties arise.

That is achieved through a model, much like the Marines, of gradual release or increased trust. Think about a coach who has a team full of individuals. Sports are also a performance based practice. They require certain skill sets to be successful. You will notice a coach getting to know their players. They understand what motivates the players and the level of each one. Practices and drills are then tailored to meet the needs of not where the coach wants the players to be, but where they actually are. That's understood by the players as respect for them as individuals and trust in their ability to improve, and not be overwhelmed by the wrong level of expectations.

We can all improve if we have the desire, understanding, and opportunity. We make this happen by getting to know those we lead, but also keeping a coaching relationship. We do this by providing timely, specific feedback that is targeted to the educator's level of development, clear expectations, and an understanding that improvement is required. Starting with high involvement for those teachers beginning or at a low performance level to less direct guidance for those performing at a higher level. It is important to understand that all teachers, no matter their level of performance, need support. We often do some of our highest performing educators a great disservice by saying they are doing a great job and moving to the next task. A successful coach never stops making small adjustments. The Marines are successful because they never stop targeting what needs improving.

EXERCISE

To really put this coaching aspect into practice, you need to start adjusting your mindset away from most evaluation systems and towards a system of support and growth. Many evaluation systems are based on what is occurring and how well the person being evaluated is progressing toward their goals. This type of system reinforces the philosophy of evaluating what has happened rather than what can happen. It is based on lag (those measurements that take stock at only a few points on the way to reaching a goal) rather than lead (a more frequent, meaningful, and flexible set of check-ins on the way to meeting a goal) indicators. After all, if the person is progressing toward their goals wouldn't that be evident in the evaluation of their practice? But if a person hasn't met their goal, isn't it too late to adjust along the way based on flexible needs?

The purpose of this exercise is to adjust our mindset from lag to lead indicators when supporting our teachers. To do that we need to meet our teachers where they are in the process of development and performance. Following the steps below will assist in building a coaching mindset focusing on lead rather than lag indicators. Once it is completed a few times, teachers will automatically start expecting not just a reflection on where they need to improve, but the support they require to do so.

ACTION STEPS

1. Look at your list of staff members or their evaluations and split that list into three levels of performance. It doesn't matter what you label them or how you measure the qualifications for each. Just make sure that the list has a high, medium, and low skill/performance level. The

reason I combine skill and performance together is because it is quite possible you can have a high skill level teacher with low performance. That is a topic for later. For the purposes of this exercise they can be combined.

2. Select one person from each list and write down one of their strengths as an educator. Reflect on how they can improve in that area. This will allow you to begin building trust and confidence when you speak with them.

3. Informally observe that educator in action and note where their strength comes out and one of their areas of need.

4. Meet within 24 hours (preferably face to face, maybe through a voice feedback tool[4], but never through email) with that person to discuss the observation.

5. Explain how you appreciate their strength and make a suggestion of how they may be able to make it even a little stronger. Then using that area of strength as a springboard, ask to reflect on how they could apply it to the areas of need you noticed.

6. End the conversation with a question as to how you can support them in shoring up that area of need.[5] Then ask for (or even schedule) a time where you can come observe them putting that improvement into practice. Doing this will help move from ideas of support and improvement to action on future iterations of the practice based on the individual context.

CREATE A MAP

"When a man does not know what harbor he is making for, no wind is the right wind." — Seneca

I can still remember standing in front of the professor with my project in hand and the question that just left my mouth. "Is it done?" I asked as I handed it toward him. "I don't know, is it?" he responded. Having yet to win my battle with perfectionism at that time in my life, my stomach did a flip and I quickly pulled the project back. "What do you mean?" I asked. His response was straightforward, but offered no guidance. He explained that I should just hand it in when I thought I had accomplished the goal of creating a long term assignment that would meet the varied learning styles in my class. While there was a goal present, its vagueness of no parameters of what success actually looked like was very difficult for me.

It created additional, unnecessary stress. I took what I had done home and put it through another few iterations before finally handing it in at the last minute because I had no more time to do it again. In retrospect, I probably could have handed it in the first time and not wasted the extra effort had I been provided some benchmarks or a clearer vision of success.

One of the largest obstacles early explorers faced was the absence of accurate maps as they journeyed to the ends of their known world. For some, this was an exciting venture with promises of glory and gold, but for others it was a fearful prospect that often ended in tragedy. The best way these individuals could have been supported in their risk taking, besides increased funding, was to have the most accurate maps possible along with some small, guiding check-ins along the way to both adjust for their needs at that time and provide insight that they were heading in the proper direction of the desired result. Similarly, one of the best ways for a leader to support those who follow is by providing a clear destination with a few guidelines along the way. One of the biggest impediments to teachers taking risks with new instructional strategies is strict adherence to process rather than clarity of outcome. Without a clearly articulated destination, there will be a lack of support in the execution of or creativity in the process.

I have found that this type of tight (vision), but loose (process) guidance is easier to implement by following a process of communication, feedback, and modeling.

COMMUNICATION

"Communication is not just about support and kindness; sometimes it's about progress and productivity." – Alan Stein Jr.

Remember that while being direct isn't about being mean or rude, it is often still uncomfortable. That's ok. We often need to be uncomfortable to learn and in the long run it is better to have a clear understanding than wasting time by guessing about expectations. The difficulty about communication is that it is often received through a filter unknown to the communicator. As a result, interpretations of the same message vary, not just from person to person, but also the context in which they were received. Supportive communication must be a clarifying experience. Teachers will need a variety of levels of support, but in an effort to create more efficient methods of supporting we often group them into a few different categories.

It is essential that the leader make certain the teacher not just understands the destination, but also their role in it when offered support.

That step allows them ownership in creating their personal map to success. The inefficient and often ineffective method of doing this is to give the vision, have a heavy hand in the plan, and then offer support based on the leader's understanding of where the teacher will struggle. A better way is when the leader communicates the vision, helps the teacher create a map that they control, and then supports the teacher based on their personal needs according to their plan. True, it is scary for the leader to let go of this much control, but doing so allows authentic, personalized support that increases the rate of improvement and engagement. As long as the destination is the original vision laid out by the leader, progress is in the near future. All that is needed is finding where the teacher needs support along the way. That comes through a continuous feedback and modeling loop.

FEEDBACK

Unfortunately, many in the field of education immediately think of a negative evaluation process when they hear the word feedback. Whether it is a formal write up or an informal walk-through, we still tie the idea of "this can be written down and go in my file" mentality. This thought process erodes trust and creates an environment geared toward crisp directives instead of a creative, personalized process toward growth. This is not to say that these methods should not occur. Instead, I believe they should all be a part of a larger discussion concerning what a teacher needs to grow. Leaders should work to understand the skill level of the teacher and base observations, conferences, and level of feedback on that information. Doing so allows them to differentiate support based on level of need. No matter the level of the educator, start by finding something that allows them to see that you understand what they are doing is not easy. In fact, if they are truly growing it will be uncomfortable and often difficult. Personally, the goal for me is to never have a teacher think I believe it's easy and they are just inadequate. This often comes in the form of a personal story or example of when I struggled with something similar. As leaders we all have had struggles in many different areas. It is our responsibility to show how those relate in a manner that makes our teachers realize that the need for support is not a personal failure, but instead an opportunity for growth. This takes vulnerability on the part of a leader, but the benefits are enormous.

These conversations should end with a recognition of the areas for support and some suggestions for one to three small actions that are relatively easy to execute, but might help. Specifically designed to give the teacher a few "easy wins", these steps must be observed in action and then followed up with a conversation. The observation of the steps are to make sure that the teacher is getting what they need. The conversation is to either adjust to some other area or larger steps now that the smaller ones have worked. The key to this conversation is to praise and encourage the teacher even if the improvement only helped a little.

Remember that while we depersonalize the struggle the teacher is having, it is important to then personalize the success.

Praise the teacher for what they did as a professional and encourage them to continue their efforts because lasting change takes time. The cycle of an observation with focused feedback on only a few items followed by supportive, honest conversations will allow a stronger, trusting relationship to be built.

MODELING

As you read this, and even as I write it, visions of broken conversations, misunderstood communication, and negative feedback come to mind. Even more so the frustrating, antagonistic relationship that begins to develop when teachers feel as if you are not being clear and you feel as if what you are communicating is simple and they just do not want to listen. Even if you continue with a positive mindset, there comes a time when improvement must occur and it is the role of leaders to support every level of teacher through that process. Each person we lead is different and has different strengths. We sometimes forget that the further we move away from the classroom and in our push to move forward. There are those who are great at classroom management, but struggle with paperwork. Some teachers are incredible working with students in person, but fall short when it comes to integrating technology. Let's not forget about the individuals who continually try new instructional strategies, but follow no plan for lessons or sometimes grading structure. You will become much more successful at knowing, communicating with, and working with your individual teachers based on their personal needs if you model your expectations. The best part about modeling is that you can do it in a number of ways.

Many times it's new technology that teachers are unsure of trying. Consider creating a video using Loom or Screencastify showing them how to use the new tool. In fact, short videos are very helpful for clarifying your expectations. It is low risk and an asynchronous method of learning. The pressure of watching it in front of you is gone and it lives forever. Teachers can go back to watch it at any time that is convenient for their schedule. Leaders can also curate other instructional videos and provide them to teachers so a library is created. One caution concerning this strategy is to make certain you set parameters, explain them, and stick to them before making this type of resource. If you say they are short, interesting, or connect to more in depth resources, make sure they do.

Another way to model is in person. Help lead a class to show that activity or non-verbal strategy you use. Make sure that the teacher is comfortable with something like this occurring. Approach it as an option for the teacher rather than saying you will show them. Sometimes the person you are trying to support may end up feeling embarrassed or self-conscious in a situation like this. Another way to accomplish this technique is to use the other experts in your building. Think about how much more powerful it is for students to see their peers doing or saying something. The same holds true for teachers. If a teacher is struggling, pair them up with another person in the building who is reaching your expectations. Do whatever you need (cover their class, get a substitute, have an in-house field trip) to get them in their colleague's classroom so they can observe your expectations in action. Often, that is all that is needed to create understanding. One extra little piece to this: Do not get hung up on the idea of making sure teachers observe each other in the same subject. Good teaching is good teaching no matter the content.

REFLECT

Now it's time to get a little vulnerable with your biggest critic, yourself. Step back and think about those teachers who continually underperform based on your expectations. The conversations with them have been difficult and you have the same mindset whenever you meet with them. You hope it is over soon and smile afterwards because you are one more meeting closer to fulfilling the required number. Have you, as a leader, ever stopped to think that the teacher either feels the same way about you or actually wants to do a better job? What if they think you just don't like them? If that's the case, how can you ever expect them to improve? Stop reading, take some time, and think about these questions and your role in teachers' failure or improvement.

1. Have I clearly communicated my expectations to them in a way that they, not me, understand?
2. Have I had frequent conversations concerning where they need improvement and how I can best support them?
3. Have I offered resources, modeled, or provided a mentor to help them begin to build momentum towards my expectations?
4. Do I honestly believe that if they could do better they would and have I put that belief into action?

Remember that most of us will quickly say that we have done all of these things to better support those we serve, because of our own confirmation bias. That's why the most important aspect of these questions has been left out, but must be addressed if we are to consider our answers honest. We tend to look at data so let's take this chance to examine what it says about us. Go back to your answers and simply look for evidence by asking and then answering "how" using specific examples.

CROSS THE GAP

"A bend in the road is not the end of the road...unless you fail to make the turn."
– Helen Keller

Once a leader has engaged the teacher in the creation of their own map, it is up to them to begin taking the trip to getting better alongside the educator. This is another way to best support, build trust, and create a relationship that allows each of you to be vulnerable and grow as both professionals and people. You both have the plan to grow, but there will be obstacles along the way. This is especially true for the teacher who is taking a forced risk because there is a clear need for improvement. Often, the teachers will soon realize that there is a gap between where they want to be as a next step in acting on their plan. When this occurs, because it will, leaders must be ready to address it before the teacher decides to return to the comfort of staying the same.

The first step in this situation is to identify and actually focus on the gap between where the teacher currently is and where they have expressed a desire or plan to be at this point in time. The important part is to not focus on what they have done wrong or all the things that are not working. This sustains the negative mindset of failure and is detrimental to progress. Instead, try using something similar to the following:

"We know that we were hoping you would be implementing <blank> at this time, but that isn't where you are. That means we have to adjust our plan. Let's talk about what you need to help you achieve <blank> and get back on track."

The idea is to focus on the difference that needs to be made up between what is and what was supposed to be. What follows are some action steps that will foster a positive, but firm process that helps move you through a difficult conversation to meaningful growth.

ACTION STEPS

1. Start the conversation by acknowledging the purpose of the conversation, reinforcing that you believe in continuous improvement, and stating you value their skill as an educator and their place in the culture of the building. This will help preserve and continue to build trust in the relationship even through a difficult conversation.

2. Focus on the gap between where the teacher needs to be and where they currently exist or perform. Identify and depersonalize what is not working.

3. Discuss the challenges the teacher is currently having with the plan they helped create. Tease out what is working, not working, and collaborate on some adjustments or action steps that may help them move forward. Create a coaching or mentoring plan to support them in closing the identified gap and improving their practice.

4. Follow up on the plan you have created in a consistent, positive manner. The best way to support a teacher is by offering meaningful feedback as close to any observation as possible. Personally, I have had great luck with doing this. Some teachers respond and some don't, but they all hear it and realize that I am there to support them in their journey.

5. Give it some time and then repeat the process.

The most important thing to remember as you move through working with teachers is to consider their perspective and believe that if they could be performing better they would. If you are insincere with your support at any point, those you lead will know and the trusting relationship you seek will never be built.

SUPPORT CHALLENGE

You have read a lot about support and the importance of making sure you are providing it to every level of teacher you have in the building. Keeping in mind that support is an active aspect of leadership, I offer you, reader, this challenge: Find three teachers who are in need of a coaching approach. Focus on continuous support by finding some way to use almost instant personalized feedback and use it regularly. Schedule follow up conversations focused on everyone leaving with an increased understanding or new point of view around their practice. Finally, model your expectations through direct instruction, colleague observations, or both.

VIGNETTE

At the midpoint of every school year the teachers in my building receive the email from me reminding them that it is time to schedule our 15 minute meeting, my administrative assistant will be setting them up, and of the three questions:

1. What am I currently doing that I need to stop?
2. What am I currently not doing that I need to start?
3. What is one thing I can do to make your life easier or better?

I then proceed to meet with every teacher and take notes on what they answer. I sit and listen without taking offense, getting defensive, or making excuses. I inform all of them that this is their opportunity to evaluate me at the halfway mark so that I can make adjustments or continue on the current course. I get a wide range of answers about what is working or not working for them. It would be dishonest to say this worked perfectly when I first started or that everything is great now, but that isn't the point. The point is for me to make time to honestly listen to every teacher in the building. The point is for me to let them know I am there to support them by genuinely asking what they have, need, and want.

What builds capacity around this practice is the action I take after my meetings. Whether it is getting a set of magnetic poetry (small money for a large return), improving communication around walking staff meetings, or noticing trends requiring larger, faculty wide discussions, I make sure to act on what I am told.

Voice doesn't matter if it isn't heard and acted upon.

In other words, I respond to the answers I receive in a noticeable way. These meetings have started a scheduling committee to adjust our school schedule, a new weekly communication[6] to the faculty, and new clubs and organizations for students. Teachers have warmed to the idea that they have my undivided attention to give me a gauge of what is working for them and how I can improve. Not everyone has an interest in meeting with me, but those individuals are few and they know there is always the opportunity. Overall, this practice has been incredibly valuable in building trust and informing me as to how I may better support my teachers. I highly recommend every leader try it in some fashion.

WISE PRACTICES AND TOOLS

Before reading this section it is important to understand that the critical aspect for any of what follows to be successful is the existence of ongoing professional conversations. Because it's important to support teachers at all levels of performance, each of these practices will look different; much like all of the students in front of us are different. These conversations must be authentic and welcome vulnerability around topics such as personal and professional challenges, limitations and benefits of the current leadership style, and needed changes. These conversations must be initiated by the leader and come from a place of genuine curiosity. Truly supporting teachers requires an open mind and ongoing discussions where everyone leaves with an increased understanding of each other's personal context and point of view.

PEER OBSERVATIONS: Hand select peers that your teachers who need support can observe. Remember that good teaching is good teaching. It doesn't need to be the same subject. Be careful not to ask them for any type of positives and negatives about what they saw when you follow up with them. Doing so will erode trust. Just ask for confirmation and what they are going to try differently in their class. It is important for leaders to support all teachers and not just those struggling. Give the whole staff the opportunity to observe their peers by offering class coverage. Doing this allows you to support teachers' strengths while at the same time assisting with teachers' needs. If you want to take it to the next level with increased, building-wide visibility, try the Pineapple Chart[7] or some other method that allows teachers to opt in and is a visible representation of what is occuring in the building.

FREQUENT INFORMAL OBSERVATIONS: Otherwise known as walkthroughs, this is a 5-7 minute observation with personalized feedback within 24 hours. I accomplish this by scheduling two blocks in my calendar each day for this one task. I use the walkie-talkie app Voxer. The best aspect of this tool is that it is free, the recipient (teacher) doesn't need to sign up to receive the message, and it is simple to use. I walk out the door, pull out my phone, and speak my observations and feedback into the app. I hit send and the teacher gets a recording of my voice offering feedback and a question. I always ask a question to encourage reflection and conversation. If you don't use something like Voxer, be sure to follow up in person as much as possible for a more meaningful, trust building interaction.

MEANINGFUL FEEDBACK: It's very important to provide honest, authentic feedback to teachers of all levels. As leaders, we sometimes try to make things sound a little nicer or quite the opposite and focus on the negative when offering feedback. All feedback must be presented in a fashion that targets the performance and developmental level of the educator. Make certain that all your feedback, positive or negative, is specific; containing examples of not just what needs to change, but how to make it happen. A way to do this is to highlight some positives and then drill down to a few goal oriented, incremental action steps toward improvement. To be effective, feedback must be clear around expectations, but supportive in execution.

MODELING: There will always be a time when those you are trying to support just don't understand what you are asking. You can either explain it a different way, realize that some people learn better visually, or see the value of observation when dealing with a complex topic. This is when it's important to model your expectations. Modeling can come in a number of ways. If a teacher needs support with an instructional strategy, the leader can teach a portion of their class utilizing that strategy. Sometimes there is a need that affects performance, but isn't directly tied to how instruction is delivered. This often pertains to organizational or presentation tools. I have found that using tools such as Loom[8] or Screencastify[9] work very well to do this because it not only models what you are explaining, but it lives on for repeated, asynchronous access by the teacher wanting guidance in that area. This lends itself to the creation of a library for you to use whenever the need arises.

PROFESSIONAL DEVELOPMENT: This is an area that is rife with missed opportunity. All too often, professional development comes in a one size fits all fashion because it is mandated from the district level or an afterthought thrown together. Every day leaders expect teachers to personalize instruction for students who need support. There is no reason we should not be doing the same for them. Specific, targeted professional development activities should be located, created, and/or provided for teachers throughout the year. These activities should include avenues for relicensure, be provided by a combination of outside providers and inside professionals, and be ongoing. A great resource to assist in accomplishing this is SimpleK12.[10]

Professional development should be the product of expressed or discovered need if teachers are going to engage in a meaningful way.

If not, no matter the topic, it is a waste of money and time. See what your teachers need, find experts in your building, bring outsiders into your building, or send your people out to other opportunities. There are times where a leader may have to get creative to provide additional time. I use substitutes, in-house field trips, faculty meetings, late starts,[11] and department meetings to accomplish providing ongoing, bite-sized professional development.

CELEBRATION: I cannot express how important it is to celebrate teachers as both people and professionals. One of my first surveys asked them their favorite snack. I then worked to put that in their mailbox on their birthday or other occasion. We begin each faculty meeting with gratitude; doing shoutouts for each other. I start my weekly administrative meetings with "personal wins". Those are just some examples of celebration. I try to publicly highlight whenever a teacher succeeds at something important to them. I also make note of when to not highlight a teacher to the rest of the faculty or community.

Some people are private or modest and that must be respected if you are truly supporting them. Those individuals are celebrated in a more quiet way through notes, personal conversations, and small acts. This is an area where it's important that things are put in writing for the exact reason all your feedback should be written. Unfortunately, many individuals live by the mantra "it doesn't count if it isn't in writing". So, as leaders we are responsible to make this limitation work for us. Just as we build trust by not putting all our feedback in writing, we build relationships and support by making sure all our celebrations are in writing.

ONE LAST THING OR MAYBE FIVE

RESISTANCE

When attempting to support those you lead, you will run into resistance. Just like a student, teachers will resist many of your attempts until they can experience the positive benefit of them. However, this takes time along with the ability to overcome fear. If you are in the position of supporting a struggling teacher, they have already been dealing with falling short. How can they expect to be better or admit your ideas and suggestions will help them if they haven't been able to do it themselves? Authentically supporting teachers is difficult enough without the added aspect of resistance when you confront them. This is why it's crucial to understand that many times resistance isn't necessarily someone trying to cause trouble. It is merely them saying they don't understand or need more support. This is often difficult for people to admit because it creates a sense of shame or fear that they are somehow inadequate. Therefore, it is easier to resist and have you not support them than suffer perceived embarrassment.

VALUE

The support we offer teachers always matches the level at which we value them as both people and professionals. No matter how hard we believe we are trying, we will only support teachers as much as we value them. First, the effort we put into anything (exercise, friendships, scheduling, etc.) is directly related to how much we value that thing. For example, if a leader sees a person as a five on a scale of 1 to 10 that means the effort they're going to expend in an effort to support them will only be a five. It will never be the 10 that it should be. Unfortunately, this level of support transfers into the classroom. Second, those we interact with realize how much we care and that directly affects the trust needed to create a supportive relationship. Leaders often need to form a new perspective around a person's acceptance or refusal of assistance when it is offered. Like teaching a subject, when supporting someone, we often default to the style that works best for us. This may lead to frustration and burnout on the leader's part because we begin to blame the recipient and look for reasons our efforts are falling short. When in reality, we are not speaking the language to which they are most receptive. Instead we speak in one that's most comfortable for us because we fail to perceive on a deeper level that supporting someone else has nothing to do with us. Sincerely value your people if you hope to be successful.

CULTURE

A positive culture based on reflection and continuous improvement creates a supportive environment for teachers. This type of culture is created through the consistent support of taking risks in teaching strategies, celebrating progress instead of perfection, and actions that show the leader is there to coach teachers up rather than evaluate them out. Any career, but especially one in education should not be filled with concern for keeping a job. Instead the concern should be about how to continually get better through coaching, meaningful feedback, and purposeful action.

EXPECTATIONS

It is important to not make the mistake of thinking that support is about lowering expectations. It is about keeping your expectations, but getting your hands dirty in helping those you lead reach them. I am often asked a question about retaining or letting teachers go for performance based issues once people hear I am a teacher-centered leader. It comes from the premise that support contains excuses. My very consistent answer is as follows. We are all in the business of education. How then, can we justify not doing everything we can to teach a teacher to get better at their craft much like we expect them to support student learning? Yes, there comes a time when that difficult decision concerning a teacher's willingness or ability to continue in your building has to be made, but only after all methods and manner of support have been exhausted. I can give that answer for two reasons. First, I actively work to support teachers no matter the issue. Second, teachers have students in front of them who are someone's child. Their most prized possession whose learning we have been entrusted with. The culture and teachers in my school must be one in which I would feel good about having my own students present.

RESOURCES

It should go without saying that once a leader is able to identify what support a teacher needs, they should do whatever it takes to provide that for them. Whether it is making sure they have access to quality professional development, updated curriculum, the appropriate feedback they need around instructional strategies and assessment, or just the time to make sense and use of everything at their fingertips to give students the best educational experience possible, it must become the mission of the leader to provide the opportunity for teachers to be the best. Leaders need to be the ultimate resource because no matter the situation, teachers need someone on their side who will listen, make suggestions, and believe in them.

REFLECT ON SUPPORT

Central to all of these situations and supporting teachers is making myself actively available as an approachable, trustworthy resource. With those who may be missing the mark, it is important to be consistent in following up, checking in, and reaffirming the authenticity of the support or relationship that allowed the conversation in the first place.

Reflection, being key to enhancing future iterations of a particular project or practice, must be modeled if expected from those we lead.

Take some quiet time to reflect on the following questions:

1. Have you ever resisted change or an initiative? How would you feel if everyone watching you labeled you as a trouble maker or crazy for resisting?
2. How many times do you find yourself not trusting or having the ability to talk about trust with a staff member and as a result you talk about them to others instead of talking to them about what they needed?
3. What systems (or behaviors) do you have in place to support those teachers that come to mind in the first two questions?

KEY TAKEAWAY

Much like the concerns my wife and I had with our son and his respiratory issue, leaders must come to a point where they concentrate on the causes of a teacher struggling rather than the symptoms if they want to create long term success or "fixes". In the beginning we listened to the referral of our pediatrician because we trusted him. In fact, we trusted him so much that the new doctor already had credibility with us because of who referred him. The new doctor continued to build that trust by holding a lengthy, initial meeting (two hours) where he had an objective, honest conversation with us. More importantly he listened to our concerns and the goals we hoped to reach.

Much like leaders helping those who need support, he worked to coach us through the barrage of appointments, tests, and sometimes confusing results with which we were about to be faced. Teachers, especially those who are struggling, often face an overwhelming amount of issues that hinge on their ability to improve. If a leader continues to throw strategies and requirements at them without coaching them through the struggle of improvement, they are almost certain to continue to struggle, if not fail altogether. They don't necessarily need someone to listen to their struggles, but instead a person who will recognize the issues and assist them in learning strategies to help them move forward. This often takes the creation of a map that includes various pathways to move forward based on results achieved along the journey.

Supporting people is not a one time event; especially in the field of education. It takes a constant loop of feedback, modeling, adjusting, planning, and then more feedback. It is imperative for leaders to not only pinpoint the cause of a teacher's need, but also create a map and the means to get to the destination by identifying the steps needed along the way. There will be times those you lead struggle against your efforts. That is not a time to ease away from your work to support, but instead hold fast to your expectations. Nobody likes to struggle and admit they need support. It often comes with feelings of inadequacy or embarrassment. Often, that shows itself in the form of resistance.

It would be easy to walk away from those who resist your efforts to support when they are falling short of your expectations or struggling in some other manner. Leadership is not easy. If you walk away from supporting others in the face of adversity, you need to reexamine the expectations you have of yourself and then, much like your teachers, get some support to improve. This is where modeling and trust play a key role. Those you serve will see you working to improve and repeated efforts to help in an authentic manner will eventually engage them in the process. Once teachers get engaged, they become key players in the overall success of the students and school. Let's look at ways to do just that.

ENDNOTES

[1] She notes that this activity is often used with a live audience. It has been effective and transferable enough that it is also mentioned in her book Dare to Lead.

[2] Brown, Brené. Dare to Lead (p. 215). Random House Publishing Group. Kindle Edition.

[3] Voxer allows me to record and provide a voice memo with feedback to the teacher as soon as I leave their room. I just take out my phone, record my thoughts, and email the teacher. The voice component is important. It is personalized and there is no guessing about tone or meaning. Teachers can receive the voice memo even without an account. I explain more in the "Wise Practices and Tools" section.

[4] This could be a voice memo, video, or any other method that allows tone and expression to be clearly understood.

[5] Sentence stems have been added to the "tools" section to help with this.

[6] This is the Panther Update. It is released every Wednesday morning using SendFox. It contains updates, reminders, resources, motivational quotes, a check-in form, and a burning question form. I use SendFox to see what teachers click on the most so I may adjust based on their interest.

[7] The Pineapple Chart is a chart hung in a visible place where teachers put what they are doing in their classes so other teachers can select where they want to go to view different instructional strategies taking place. A lesser version is that teachers who welcome colleagues to observe hang a pineapple or some other symbol on their door as a sign of welcome.

[8] Loom is a web-based screen recording tool that is very helpful for explaining how to use programs on the computer. You are able to record your voice (picture of yourself optional) as you move through the steps a teacher would need. It is the creation of an instructional video with your voice.

[9] Screencastify is the same type of tool as Loom, but is the free Google extension. In the name of full transparency, I prefer using Loom.

[10] SimpleK12 is a software resource that my district has just recently purchased. It is a vast library of webinars that cover everything from SEL, podcasting, tech integration, leadership, and more. It does cost, but is definitely worth checking out for the price.

[11] We start students one hour later every other Thursday. This time is used by teachers to work on curriculum, cover instructional strategies, analyze student work, peer coach, meet with mentors, etc.

ENGAGE

In for a penny, in for a pound.
Brian McCann

While the origin of the quote starting this section lies in 17th century literature, I attributed it to Brian McCann[12] for two reasons. First, he embodies what it means. You will never find Brian using half measures or "mailing it in" so to speak. If he decides to get involved, he is in all the way. Everything from Brian's work ethic to his final delivery of product screams engagement. Second, because he unknowingly called me out on something that I was working on using this phrase. In fact, he didn't even finish the phrase. All that sat on that reply to one of my tweets was "In for a penny...". I had offhandedly sent a reply to one of his pictures on Twitter. It showed him with a whole video set up (ring light, microphone, etc.) to record his virtual presentation for a conference at which we had both been accepted to present. I mentioned him going overboard in his normal fashion. Normally, his reply was typical Brian and I at first scrolled by it. But this time, reading it sent a very personal message home to me. I had been accepted to present at a conference during the pandemic. While I had done plenty of presentations before, this one was virtual. I was a little concerned about building a presentation and talking to the computer screen for people to look at later, but I decided to give it a try. I don't know where the disconnect was. I record weekly videos to my community and deliver engaging messages. This seemed different and I struggled with my level of engagement. As that struggle continued, my typical energy waned and the product wasn't as good as it could have been. I found my presentation to be stiff with almost a scripted feel. It was clearly because I was frustrated with the process that seemed impersonal, but I had not taken any extra measures to mitigate that feeling. The end result was that I had fallen short of putting myself all in to engage others in a presentation I was giving. The question that nagged me was how could I ever expect to get people engaged in what I had to say or do if I wasn't there myself? Simply put, I was not giving my maximum effort to have the largest positive impact possible and knowing this had just become too clear to be comfortable. I may never present virtually again due to my comfort level and knowledge of how I struggled with it in the past. I may not even be given the opportunity. However, I do know this, if I am in the situation where I can face that obstacle again, I will understand the importance of being fully engaged from the beginning until the end. Those on the receiving end deserve nothing less and it is up to me to deliver.

We all want to be good leaders. Hopefully, we all want to be great leaders. But to be great we have to have the largest possible impact. This takes a few things like continuous improvement, a dedication to learning as much as possible, and finally a true belief in and understanding of the following phrase:

Your impact as a leader is directly tied to the motivation and commitment of those you serve.

So how do leaders increase motivation and commitment? Personally, I achieve this through engagement. I continuously work to achieve engagement through three major strategies: knowledge of those I lead, personalization, and promotion. They work because of what they produce for those I lead.

Ultimately, people become engaged for three reasons. First, they relate to the vision in which they are involved. The less a person relates, the more what they are doing feels like a job rather than a calling. Second, a sense of belonging exists. All people have a need to feel as if they are valued for their contribution to the larger group. If this is missing, there is a distinct pulling away as feelings of isolation creep into their existence. Finally, individuals become more engaged when they see the product of their labors. Anything anyone ever works on is much more engaging when the outcome is tangible as they progress. Consider all the weight loss ads that promise so many pounds off in a short time frame or that the dieter can see the fat just "melt away." While these may not work as advertised, most people stay with these programs as long as they see measured progress. They are engaged. Achieving one of these three will yield results, but a leader needs all three if they are to achieve the largest possible impact on those they lead.

CONNECTION TO VISION

We were on the third step in our "Connecting to Our Why" activity. Faculty members started by watching and listening to me model my thought process around my why and how it incorporated my core values. As an aside, I'm glad I performed this exercise because of the clarity it provided as my why turned into what Simon Sinek has termed a "Just Cause" in his book *The Infinite Game*.[13]

> ## My just cause is to improve the educational experience for everyone involved by being purposeful, acting with integrity, and building character.

But in staying with the faculty aspect, I modeled this and then had them identify theirs for the express reason of personal identification and the sharing of knowledge. Moving to the second step, they gathered as small groups to share the reasons they entered education, ways they made certain they were being true to that, and obstacles they faced each day. In essence, teachers were asked to explain why they had drifted (if they had) away from their original passions that engaged them in the profession and what they needed to overcome to get back. This was great information for me, as their leader, to use for improving the culture. Finally, as the last step, the staff gathered into three large groups, shared some of their passions and roadblocks, and then created a short story explaining their current positions as a group. They were expected to explain who they were, what they had become, and why.

While a little awkward for some at first, they spoke their stories. There became a clear theme as to who we were as a group, what we wanted to be, and what was needed to assist in getting there. In short, we came up with a sort of vision (who we want to be) and a mission (what we need to do to get there) that could be refined later. More importantly, it was everyone's story and they were all connected. Remember those areas or tools for engagement I mentioned earlier? After this exercise I now had a working knowledge (everything was written down and turned into me) of what really mattered to people and what they perceived to be holding them back. It was a personalized experience that I could later promote during communications and reflection on decisions.

The promotion or reflecting back to the reasons we had created this is what's most important. Not just for the idea of valuing the time, effort, and product of those you serve, but because to truly feel connected, teachers need to see and understand the so-called bigger picture. Having clarity around the goals and purpose of the school builds engagement among staff. When people understand and have a part in creating the greatest priorities concerning culture, student learning, and community responsibility, to name a few, for a building, changes focused on overall improvement in those areas are not just accepted, but embraced. Sure, this all sounds like common sense, but for many reasons it is not common practice. Think about how many times visions, missions, initiatives, and school improvement plans are dictated to the many by the few. If leaders want a high level of engagement in their school, they must let those who are most affected create it through ownership.

Yes, leaders must work to create engagement, but utilizing knowledge of those you serve, personalization, and promotion allows the ownership aspect to be transferred; thus creating an even stronger sense of engagement. Many top districts and schools in the area of culture and student success have this process in place. They have a common vision about what's best for students, the school community, and teachers. They know what they want it to look like, what barriers they will and currently face, how they will overcome them by focusing on the future, and engaging in the work. Working through this lens creates an environment of continuous improvement.

Oftentimes the idea of continuous improvement becomes daunting for people. They approach it with a mindset that focuses on the idea they have to get better.

This is why the leader must make it clear that continuous improvement is not about not being good enough, but instead

imagining how much better a person can be by just moving the needle by one or two percent.

This is where personal knowledge of those you serve comes into play. No matter how hard you try, you cannot engage a person without having knowledge of their interests and needs. People are unique and as a result have different interests, motives, and aspirations. I used the exercise described above, but I also personally gain this knowledge through surveys and feedback. It's important to give surveys that collect the various needs, desires, interests, and concerns to staff. This allows your attempts to engage to be focused and timely. Once you have the information, you are able to ensure a more engaging workplace because a majority of the guesswork is eliminated.

A second method I use to gain knowledge is collecting feedback. I categorize this differently from surveys because I engage people face to face for feedback. When I say feedback I am not talking about you giving it to someone else. Rather, I am talking about opening yourself up to those you lead. The crucial aspect of this is making sure that you listen and accept feedback for what it is without defending, justifying, or explaining the feedback you receive. This gives those you lead the opportunity to see that they are able to have a direct involvement in your actions that affect them. That's pretty engaging.

REFLECTION

How does the knowledge you have of your staff fit into the crafting of a vision that they personally connect with, makes them belong, or helps them see their success? Take some time here to write down ways you have attempted to get better at this. What worked? How can you do it better? Now take some time to write down some new ways you will try moving forward.

ACTION STEPS

1. Select 5-7 different staff members to have a conversation about vision.
2. Use the conversation to gain knowledge about them as a person and their connection to the vision.

3. Discern what their level of engagement is and why?

4. Create a personalized three-step plan to connect (or reconnect) them to the broader vision of the school. Hint: you have already done the first by meeting with them.

BELONGING

Once you have the knowledge of what people need, take the next step by not just personalizing their experience, but connecting them to the larger group. I call this the "I'm not alone in this" feeling. I equate this to any other type of strenuous activity we perform in an attempt to improve ourselves. I'll use exercising as an example. Many of us can get in better shape. So we work to improve how far, fast, or more we run, bike, or lift. This is a difficult space to exist in alone because of the little voice that lets us know nobody will notice if we don't push a little harder. We then often justify our falling short of a goal by reminding ourselves that we are doing this alone so only we truly know how we feel. What I'm saying at first sounds like a need for an accountability partner to make sure we continue to work. That's not it. I'm talking about the feeling of the workout being easier or better because someone is there with you, which keeps any of those earlier thoughts from ever entering your mind. You stop making excuses because you are engaged in the work because you belong. You have found your circle. Your personal vision or "why" fits with theirs. Looking at this from an educational standpoint again means that one more step is required. Before you can make a person feel as if they belong, you need to understand and then provide what they need to own their place in the larger vision.

Leaders often talk about the need for teachers to personalize their instruction for students. We need to do the same for our teachers. In the advent of all the social, emotional learning (SEL) strategies, this personalization includes creating an environment that takes into account the emotional state of those involved.

The point is to make sure you, as a leader, personalize things like environment, directions, and professional development, even if it is for a single staff member.

If those you lead see that you treat them and their needs individually, they will be more motivated to follow your lead. Here's the kicker: this means that you can't always follow the policy or worry about setting or following precedent whenever you make a decision. As a leader, you must be prepared to say, "the context was different and as a result needed a different solution" when you are confronted concerning the differences in your decisions. The key is to make all your decisions traceable back to the core value of individualizing based on the need of the teacher because what's good for the goose is not always good for the gander.

Once a leader makes teachers feel as if they are accepted for who and where they are as both a person and professional, the work to help them belong to the larger picture becomes one of the most important acts for building your staff into a cohesive, positive, and engaged community. This can be accomplished by explicitly helping teachers understand how they fit into the larger picture of the school community. This can be accomplished through individual meetings that start with asking how they see themselves as part of the community and build to you giving them your opinion. I work to provide articles, quotes to reflect on, and other items to support self reflection and performance. This is a more subtle, rather than explicit approach, but effective with certain staff. I learned this lesson during a staff Twitter chat around a book we were reading together, What School Could Be.[14] As we were discussing questions I was posting, (this was my first year as principal of this school) a question to one of my replies came forward and hit me right in the nose. A teacher asked if their current administration believed in what the author had written or was it just for the purpose of having a discussion. Talk about a person looking to see if they belonged! Reflecting on this was difficult for me. There I was, asking teachers to comment on ideas that were integral to where they saw themselves fitting in the larger picture. I had fallen short by not doing that work first. As a result, I changed some of my habits or I should say behaviors, in an effort to make new habits.

To make sure teachers have a clear picture to either feel as if they fit, can identify, or want to question what I believe, I adjusted the way I communicate both my own and the broader school community's vision on a consistent basis. In essence, I inform them of my personal stance at any given time much like I ask from them. This is a form of modeling, but it goes further. I share my wonderings with teachers after classroom visits. I include different articles that are relevant to what I am thinking in a weekly internal newsletter along with a quote to ponder, and weekly check in form. I also have a link where teachers can submit questions to me that they may not want to ask during a regular meeting. Working with my leadership team, I make certain communication is open by providing a spot on my agendas titled, "What did I miss?" I also bring up topics I am thinking about so everyone feels as if they have all the information and have not been left out or "not noticed". The message I send is clear. It states that I value everyone, but understand I cannot pay attention to everything. Therefore, I offer times for anyone to speak up, slow me down, and explain that their values have been possibly overlooked.

I do these things because in the end, if we are to be as successful as possible, we have to reflect on and exhibit our belief of why we are here.

An engaging culture of support and empowerment can only be achieved if everyone is led to accept ownership in its creation.

Engaging teachers is only possible if they have something they see as worthy of their time, energy, and interest. That only comes when it meshes with why they are present in the first place.

REFLECTION
How much do you know about the individual "why" of each of your staff members? How does that fit into your larger vision of "why" for the whole school? What can you do with your staff to highlight your personal why and show them that they belong to the larger community even as individuals?

ACTION STEPS
1. Create a discussion guide designed to help someone discover or explain their "why".
2. Schedule five meetings with teachers with whom you do not have a lot of interaction.

3. Use these meetings as an opportunity to learn about their why and show that they not only fit, but are a valuable part of the larger vision.
4. Refine your process and schedule meetings with the rest of your staff.
5. Create a way to cast your overall vision to the staff in a manner that is inclusive of all.

TANGIBLE OUTCOMES

Many leaders have heard of the Five Love Languages that are essential to making sure you communicate with people in a way that effectively meets their needs. While these are very helpful, they don't specifically translate to making sure teachers can see the tangible outcomes of their effort. What does transfer is the idea behind them. More and more leaders are working to recognize teachers and tell the story of their school. This is great and needs to continue, but unfortunately sometimes falls short because it hasn't met the way those we lead are most open to accepting such recognition.

I think of my staff meetings that start with what I label gratitude. They are basically shout outs for the good things I have seen throughout the building as I visit classrooms and attend events. I have practiced this for quite a few years, but it wasn't always easy. I remember the mixed reactions I first received because I hadn't considered how people like to be recognized. The end result was certain teachers gossiping in the faculty room about not being recognized and others saying they wish they hadn't been. The struggle I was experiencing in operationalizing something I knew was good was completely my fault. That is when I decided to learn more about my staff and how they liked to be recognized. Fast forward to meetings today and you will see that those who need others to recognize them get recognized even if it is something I have to specifically look for while those who do not are approached with a card, note, or in person recognition. I also make some use of recognizing the good things shyer teachers do in a "third party way." What I mean is that I will recognize a group they work with or highlight the student I saw them affect in class.

The point is that you should be bragging on your teachers, publicly celebrating what they do, and telling your school's story to the public. Do it in a way that is compatible with the comfort level of those you lead.

Once you have them motivated through the creation of an informed, personalized setting, make sure you promote any work they do that shows their level of engagement. The moment you think you are sharing too much is the moment you have just started to share at the needed level. This can come via social media with pictures, explanations, or even best; videos highlighting how awesome they are. Whichever method you choose, just make sure you use it a lot. This creates a desire to do even more by taking chances and supporting your initiatives. It also creates a positive undertone to whoever else they spend time with. They feel valued, heard, and understood. Not to mention, most people secretly like to see their picture and have people compliment them. Otherwise our social media networks wouldn't be so popular! You may be thinking to yourself that there is a lot of negativity on social media. I invite you to do what I did and turn that negativity into a positive or at least neutral force. Find the negative sites, share everything positive, and ignore the negative comments. Actually, don't ignore them. Drown them out with so much positivity that eventually the negative people stop or even better, the positive people call them out when they post a negative comment.

Finally, while all of the recognition is great, remember that we live in a "like" driven world. As a result, small steps and slow progress aren't always recognized and celebrated.

It is incredibly important as a leader to model progress not perfection with staff by taking them as individuals where they are and then highlighting how far they have come.

Recognition of work put in is important, but also requires follow up if improvement is expected to take root. Depending on how the person best accepts recognition should guide your practice here.

A strategy I like to use when doing this with people who are maybe somewhat shy, reserved, or put additional weight on the dynamic of principal and teacher is to have one of their colleagues take them aside and recognize them. It often means a little more coming from another teacher, the message that their efforts are being noticed is delivered, and you now have someone continuing to engage in the work.

REFLECTION

In what ways are you currently showing off the accomplishments of your staff? Do you take enough time to highlight individuals in the manner that best works for them? How can you improve recognizing staff accomplishments to increase engagement?

ACTION STEPS

1. Try three new ways to highlight some of your staff's tangible outcomes utilizing social media, handwritten notes, or meetings.
2. Journal about how it worked and reflect on areas to improve.
3. Try your least favorite (the one you stayed away from the first time) way of recognizing staff.
4. Add the most successful strategy to your daily or weekly routine for consistency.

ENGAGEMENT CHALLENGE

Engagement can be difficult and easily dismissed as the other person's responsibility. We don't let teachers blame students for not being engaged so why do we allow ourselves to blame the teachers? If your teachers are not engaged it isn't always a teacher problem. Sometimes it's a leadership problem. Take some time to look at your teachers' overall level of engagement. The signs are always there. How empty is the parking lot 20 minutes after dismissal? Are teachers staying more than the obligated two afternoons a week? What does attendance at extracurricular events look like? The list goes on with faculty meetings, professional development activities, and volunteer event attendance. My overall challenge for engaging teachers is to gain a deeper understanding of ways to engage your staff members by learning about, personalizing messages, and then spreading around the great work they are doing. Achieve this and I promise; you won't be disappointed!

WISE PRACTICES AND TOOLS

CONNECTING TO "WHY" ACTIVITIES: This is something that can be accomplished with something ranging from abstract field games or concrete meetings like the one described earlier. What's important is that you regularly gather staff to highlight why they are doing this work. Do not always only focus on the school vision or collective why. Use examples of individuals' whys so they can connect with how they fit into the larger group. This connection assists in engaging them with the people, school, and idea of continually improving to live their why.

SOCIAL MEDIA: Make use of every social media tool you can with a special eye towards where each of your audiences exist and craft the message you are trying to deliver accordingly. Personalized hashtags are key to doing this. Have specific hashtags that every person in your organization uses whenever they post a picture. Make sure you do the same to model your expectations. My school uses a few hashtags[16], which I collect and and then put together pictures highlighting their classroom activities using movie software[17] in a weekly video titled "Our Story". This video becomes more than just images of teachers showing what they are doing in class and around the school. Ultimately, it lifts teachers up and gives them the confidence to share their classroom story with the larger community. Putting this together can be a lot of work so make sure that you don't try to manage a social media campaign as separate acts on separate platforms. Much like Zapier[18] can be used to collect and organize information for you, find something similar to IFTTT[19] to automate the dissemination of posts to different sites for you. At the time of writing this, I find professionals on LinkedIn, Facebook, and Twitter, parents and some professionals on Facebook, parents and some students on Twitter, and Instagram, Snapchat, and TikTok are where most students are checking in regularly. If you really want to increase the engagement factor, tag the department, team members, or friends of the teacher you are bragging about in the post you put out.

INDIVIDUALIZED PROFESSIONAL DEVELOPMENT UTILIZING STAFF: Individuals are engaged in what they find personally valuable. If you want to increase teacher engagement and improvement make sure you plan professional development based on what their individual needs are at the time. The first and most obvious (or sometimes most difficult) way to accomplish this is by checking with each staff member or department's goals and then finding relevant professional development. This is a good time to utilize Department Chairs or Teacher Leaders if you have them in your building. They often have a very good handle on what is needed for support in the areas of curriculum and instruction. The other route, which is the one I prefer to utilize, is more labor intensive for the leader, but the benefits for teachers are enormous. Create mini-conference workshops utilizing the talent and knowledge you have in the building. This is a great way to empower your higher achieving teachers and engage the other teachers who either do not realize what their colleagues are doing everyday or just don't have the time to see them in action. This technique is incredibly engaging, spreads wise practices, and creates space for difficult conversations around culture and instruction.

FACULTY COMMITTEES AND PLANNING GROUPS: Normally when people hear the word committee they immediately think of a group that often gets little accomplished compared to the amount of time they take away. This is not the case if you have a few focused specifically on engaging the staff. Some that come to mind are a Professional Development, Activity, Culture, and Diversity, Equity, and Inclusion (DEI) Committees. I used names that would make clear what each of these committees does, but there are plenty of great examples of more engaging names. No matter the name, you must make sure that they are meaningful if individuals are going to be engaged. Committees that do not last past the stated time, have focused agendas, assign tasks, communicate, and follow up are the most productive. However, we are going for engagement. It is key that you accomplish what the committee plans if staff is going to be engaged. Think about it. You have a committee made up of the people you, as a leader, are trying to impact planning engaging activities. One key aspect of using specific planning groups is making sure there is diverse representation. This will allow more engagement as the involved individuals speak to their colleagues.

SURVEYS: This is an incredibly useful tool if used properly. Much like shorter videos or ones with a lot of movement hold the viewer for a longer period of time, your surveys need to be adjusted and changed up for creativity if staff is to continually participate. That is only at the surface level. When using surveys the leader must message to their people that their participation is an important way to exercise their voice and that you care about what they need. The results must then be used in a manner in which everyone knows the information came from the survey.

This will create more engagement from the staff in the next survey because you can say with confidence that you will always use the results.

SOCIAL GATHERINGS: These are important events to highlight what is important to the overall culture of the school. The stakes for these events are high because they must give everyone a sense of belonging, but as with the in-house conferences mentioned earlier, the payoff is huge. Does your staff have a holiday party, end of year softball game, or trivia night? Think about the friendships that are built and how the culture is impacted when these events are the norm. These gatherings also pose an unseen, but felt difficulty for the leader. You must have a heavy hand in making sure you create space and break down obstacles so these can occur, attend for some time, but then leave after a little while. This allows your teachers the opportunity to socialize with you in a more casual atmosphere, but also build stronger relationships and be even more casual with their colleagues once you leave. This will show them you are engaged as their leader, but respectful of their need to interact without the idea that you are watching.

RECOGNITION: This is a very important aspect of engagement. People like to be recognized, but make sure you understand what type actually engages them. I open every meeting with a section I call gratitude. It is a specific time set aside for me to give a shoutout to individuals in front of the whole faculty. Then the staff takes turns doing it for each other. This activity engages people with other individuals' lives and practice. Try this and watch it grow from week to week and month to month. Wait time and knowing your people are two tips that will help you take this practice to the next level of engagement. The Bystander Effect[20] is a very real phenomenon and is always present in faculty meetings. True to form, the larger the faculty, the more present the effect. As a result, I use wait time to my advantage. This is because the discomfort of silence outweighs the feeling that someone else will speak up.

I will wait in silence for the longest time until someone offers a shout out. Once that happens, multiple people speak up and engagement occurs. The second tip is making sure you know who does not like to be recognized in front of their peers. This will have the opposite effect and cause disengagement. We still need to engage and recognize these people, but do it in a way that fits their level of comfort and appreciation. Try little gestures such as conversations, cards, emails, etc. that show them they are appreciated.

ACTIVITY DAYS: Spending all of your time on work can be a demoralizing, divisive prospect. When was the last time those you lead did something fun, outside of the workday that included the whole staff? Take the time to plan some informal team building activities that help faculty take a break from the regularly expected, every day operations. These can be small things built into the day like department costume competitions, an ice cream social as a second half of the regularly planned faculty meeting, or a photo booth at your next professional development day. If you want to turn it up even more, plan a district-wide scavenger hunt with mixed-school teams, a hashtag contest, or an about me at home bingo board. The point is to get people involved with each other so they become more invested in the school.

NEWSLETTERS AND INTERNAL COMMUNICATIONS: The best way to engage people is to make them feel as if they are an actual important, valued part of the organization. Keep that thought in mind when I tell you that we communicate with who we think are important. Think about when something really good happens to you. Who is the first person you tell? Why? I think back to when I was offered the contract to write this book. I found out around noon and waited until I got home to tell the first person; my wife. Why? Because I want her engaged in my life; both the highs and the lows.

> **People who do not have all the information they need to feel part of the larger story naturally disengage and re-engage with something else that makes them more of an integral part.**

This is why your communication, both frequency and accessibility is key.

> **Communicate too little and people feel left out, but communicate too much and people tune out.**

65

Consistency is key because it builds expectation and satisfies people's need for predictability. Along with this, all communications need to be accessible by being clear and concise. The model I use is a weekly newsletter that goes out to my staff and the whole community. I use Smore[21] because of its ease of use. I have a template that I reuse each week and cut and paste what departments and clubs submit. I then keep my internal communications to staff to a once a week internal newsletter. I use SendFox, which I mentioned earlier, for many of the same reasons I use Smore, but it also allows me to track what people are engaging with so I can provide more of that content. The content has some crossover between the two methods, but also contains different, more detailed information for staff to show they have even more of the story, because I want them authentically engaged in its creation and continuation.

ONE LAST THING

Beware making excuses when it comes to engaging staff in anything ranging from social activities to curriculum work. Sometimes as leaders we fall victim to the notion of motivating our staff. We work to get them excited about an idea, professional development, or latest initiative only to find that momentum soon fades and additional progress becomes even harder before grinding to a halt. That is because motivation is often extrinsic and therefore reliant upon an outside source where engagement is intrinsic. Once there is engagement, people will move forward regardless of the professional or personal hurdles because they understand how whatever they are working on relates to their personal interest.

All too often it is too easy to point the finger at those who are not engaged and blame them. Stop reading right now and point your finger at any object or person near you. Now turn your hand over and look at it. I was told a long time ago that whenever I point a finger at someone else there are three pointing back at me. Do you see it now? Whatever the reason a leader gives for staff not engaging should be thoroughly examined with "so, what can I do?" questions.

Clearly, a leader often has to start with motivation through the use of various strategies, but true engagement only comes from the three areas of relation, belonging, and outcomes. These three areas are the centerpiece of intrinsic motivation, which leads to outward engagement. When a teacher feels excited or connected to an idea or practice, he or she will often go above and beyond the call of duty. As administrators, our role is both to foster conversations to help our colleagues reflect on ways to refine their ideas and serve as a resource with ideas and tools to make the idea a reality. I model this by making sure I consistently communicate what I am learning, reading, and observing to stakeholders. This strategy is meant to engage people in the overall culture of the school. Once this occurs they feel as if it is an environment where risk taking is supported and they have a role to play, they will definitely play it by taking action toward being an empowered educator.

VIGNETTE

Seriously, who gets engaged over a discussion around Tier One support strategies that are being utilized by teachers in a consistent manner in the school? At least that's what I thought until Dr. Nicole Semas-Schneeweis, our Special Education Coordinator, took over the process. Dr. Semas-Schneeweis, or Nikki as most of us call her, is the definition of engagement. Intelligent, driven, and thoughtful, Nikki has a mind that appears to be built for seeing programmatic structures and operations. She is full of energy and once she has a goal in sight there is no stopping her. This is due to the fact that Nikki not only has a clear, determined sense of doing what's right, but the ability to adjust perspective and engage others by respecting them and providing a sense of safety and belonging. She is most deservedly respected throughout our district.

This time Nikki's goal was to rewrite extraneous accommodations out of Individualized Educational Plans (I.E.P.s) that were left over from middle school based on a combination of an unfamiliarity with high school programming and a parental concern that their child needed every extra support available. Nikki realized she needed to accomplish two things to make this happen. Parents needed to feel as if their child would still be supported without the written accommodation and staff needed a voice in how this was accomplished. It started by Nikki compiling a list of all the accommodations needing to be examined. She then went to the Special Education (SPED) teachers with the list and asked what typical instruction in the classroom looked like. During this meeting, which turned into multiple, teachers specifically identified the instructional practices that were always in use for students regardless of their SPED status. Nikki then came to me with a letter she had drafted to parents.

The letter was an agreement or promise from our staff as a whole that the instructional strategies (accommodations) listed were in regular use and as a result not needed to be identified on the students I.E.P.. Her plan was to present this letter to parents at their meetings and write the strategies (all Tier 1) out of the I.E.P.s. This would give the parents the feeling of safety they needed to agree. There was just one more step to complete before using the letter. Nikki and I planned on how we would present this to the faculty to make sure they had a voice and felt comfortable. Over the course of two staff meetings the reasoning and genesis of the letter and Tier One supports were explained, the list of accommodations was examined, and teachers participated in work groups to add or subtract strategies as they saw fit.

The end result, thanks to Nikki's thoughtfulness, was full engagement by the teachers in the process, outcome, and ongoing support. Parents were comfortable ridding the I.E.P.s of unnecessary accommodations because they felt understood, teachers felt a sense of belonging in the bigger picture and had a voice, and everyone saw an end result to their efforts. Something that would have (and actually is in many schools) a difficult subject to approach and solve became easy because of increased engagement by the teachers.

REFLECT ON ENGAGEMENT

A lot of this sounds like it is about getting the right people on the bus[22]. That is only part of the engagement piece though. Often as leaders, we talk about trying to engage individuals who we did not hire, but inherited. What we need to be asking ourselves is what we are doing to make our "bus" somewhere they not only want to be, but actively contribute in a positive fashion to the journey. We will talk about actually taking the wheel next. It comes down to the fact that ultimately, teachers need to feel like the work they are doing is valued and has an impact. If you get a few teachers on board with an event and it is successful and celebrated you gain momentum for the next event.

This often sounds easy and honestly is for those who are easily engaged. However, once the excitement wears off they too will become disengaged unless you foster those feelings of connectedness, belonging, and valuable contribution.

True long lasting engagement becomes possible when there is a balance of the mirror and window philosophy. Teachers need to be able to look at a culture and see themselves, their beliefs, and what they stand for clearly represented whether it is subtle or overt. That provides the connectedness so many of us seek. They also need to be able to look at that same culture and see a different world. The possibilities that lie in the future. A future currently out of their reach, but attainable if they put in the effort with this group of people or organization. It is up to the leader to provide both viewpoints for teachers. It is all too easy to get bogged down in our everyday tasks, focusing on the very thing in front of us. I am all for being present in the moment, but am careful to look up every once in a while to make sure I see what I am part of and it is my responsibility to make sure I remind or help teachers to do the same. Consider the following story of the three masons to illustrate my point.

A medieval traveler, wandering across the country, comes across a huge construction project. Near his path, he sees three stone masons, hard at work with their hammers and chisels.

"What are you doing?" asks the traveler.
"Breaking stones," grunts the first.
"Making a wall," says the second.
"Building a cathedral!" proclaims the third.[23]

There are times where leaders, me especially, can relate to each answer. Being able to explain what I was dealing with at the time, I thought one of those ways only serves to make me believe there are times when teachers feel all three. My concern is that they often settle on the second feeling more often than the third. Let's not even talk about when they feel in line with the first response. It is my responsibility as their leader to push them ever closer to living with the third feeling. I am not an idealist and realize that every role we play comes with the fact that we have to "eat our vegetables" from time to time, but a school's or community's long term success is directly related to a leaders ability to show people that those "vegetables" are essential to their health and actually not that bad. The only problem with this story is in its delivery. People often use it to highlight attitudes and perceptions. I assert that it is about support, engagement, and empowerment. You need to support the stonecutters, engage the wall builders, and empower the cathedral builders. You can't expect others to have a broad vision without a leader and their engagement depends on you. Model and invest in building authentic relationships centered on connectedness, belonging, and recognition with those you lead. After all, who doesn't want a school full of cathedral builders. Yeah, let's talk about that next!

ENDNOTES

12 Mr. Brian McCann is the Principal of Case High School in Swansea Massachusetts. Along with being named a 2019 MassCUE Pathfinder, the 2018 National Association of Secondary School Principals (NASSP) Digital Principal of the Year, and the 2011 Massachusetts School Administrators Association (MSAA) High School Principal of the Year, he is a leader in innovative practices at the high school level.

13 (Sinek, 2019)

14 (Dintersmith, 2018)

15 The five love languages referenced are words of affirmation, gifts, acts of service, quality time, and physical touch. (Chapman, 2015)

16 The hashtags #WHPantherPride, #WHPantherPathways, and #WHArtsMatter are our main tags.

17 I use WeVideo to create this weekly movie, but I also use Animoto to create a weekly "Sports Short" movie. Make sure to identify what you are trying to accomplish and select a tool that is efficient for you.

18 Zapier is a web based service that lets you set up "Zaps" and then monitors the web for the information you are collecting. For example, I have a Zap set up so that every time the hashtag "WHPantherPride" is used, it populates a new row on a Google sheet with the user, text, and link to the tweet. This simplifies my creation of a weekly video for the newsletter about what is occurring in our school.

19 IFTTT stands for "If This Then That" and is a web based service that allows me to automate social media posts through one site. For example, I will set up an IFTTT that says if I post on Instagram, then it takes my post and puts it on twitter and facebook. This saves time by efficiently putting my message on multiple sites.

20 This is also known as bystander apathy; a theory that states individuals are less likely to offer help to a victim when there are other people present. It has many citations and examples, but the latest to me comes from The Person You Mean to Be by Dolly Chugh.

21 Smore is an online newsletter creation tool that has various paid plans, but offers discounts to educators and districts.

22 You can read more on the topic of getting the right to people on the bus in Jon Gordon's work titled The Energy Bus.

23 There have been many leadership books and talks that reference this story. It is considered an "old story" with no proper attribution.

EMPOWER

Power concedes nothing without a demand.
It never did and it never will.
Frederick Douglass

Empowerment is about taking power, influence, and authority from the people at the top and handing it to others. Or it can be about all of the same except the leader gives it to others; creating a more positive, efficient, and successful environment. While the quote opening this section did and continues to carry much more weight when originally delivered[24], the truth of the words at their face value is transferable to a struggle that teachers often face in the classroom. There are many progressive areas in education where leaders are empowering their teachers on a daily basis, but the opposite mindset still exists in too many systems to be ignored. This is not to say that all of the general resistance to the large-scale empowerment of teachers is based in the old corporate style bureaucracy. In fact, that sometimes just serves as an excuse for the local level leaders to not let go of the reins of control. It is due to the feelings illustrated in the quote above why it is absolutely essential for leaders to recognize that they must empower teachers before it is asked or even demanded of them. It becomes a choice of two roads. Voluntary empowerment, which is freely given and positive, pushes everyone to new heights of success. Empowerment that has been demanded by those seeking it ends up in confrontation and conflict. This stops the successful improvement of everyone involved.

Implicit and explicit are the two main categories of how a leader empowers their people to higher levels of success. The two often walk a fine line of being in a voluntary or involuntary situation as mentioned above. As with many things, there are plenty of gray areas built upon within the individualized needs of those in your care. Implicitly empowering someone takes the approach that they have a responsibility or desire to take the lead role in a specific situation. It comes about in the silence of the leader, which forces a response from the person being empowered. One example are those emails in which leaders are included or discussions in which you are sitting around larger issues or questions. Implicitly empowering people requires the leader to not reply to the email or sit back in the conversation and watch people figure the issues out themselves. This often creates a vacuum (or opportunity) for a person who should be and could be making the decision anyways to step forward. While implicit empowerment works well, there is an inherent risk that no one will step forward. Explicit empowerment carries very little risk of acceptance and is very powerful, but relies on the leader to properly assign responsibilities without teacher input. In other words, this is when you actively assign duties or activities to individuals. Quite possibly effective, but at the same time limiting because it leans toward the demanding aspect of empowerment.

There are many aspects to empowerment, but the most important is the marriage and modeling of the leaders' belief in and celebration of those they serve.

It requires a two way high level of trust that challenge and stress are part of the life long learning and continuous improvement process. Once this belief becomes a common aspect of the culture, there is increased momentum to take risks, try new things, and work within rather than against a changing environment. I personally work to achieve this by telling and showing teachers that I believe in them and their ability to achieve. Empowerment is most powerful when teachers believe in themselves.

A STORY OF GIVING AND DEMANDING

Sometimes we work to empower teachers, but rely on versions of empowerment that still retain significant amounts of control. This is due to how strong the subconscious feelings of control and perfection are ingrained in us as leaders. After all, these qualities often played a large role in the success we have had up until this point. These can be effective, but only to a point. I fell into this trap and once I began receiving some demands, opened it up to something I later realized was much more valuable to the community as a whole.

I continued to push to do everything I could to empower my staff in the area of professional development, but still wanted them to take the lead. What I didn't realize is that I had not taken the necessary steps (with both my staff and self) to achieve the level of success I desired. What I had planned was meant to be a stepping stone to a greater version, where the teachers would provide professional development to their colleagues. I had been touting this idea and was very vocal about us having all the expertise we needed in the building already. I listened to teachers talk about what they needed and combined those requests with what I thought we needed as a community. Once this was done I tapped certain teachers to lead those workshops. I then split the faculty into groups and rotated every member through every (three in total) workshop. I thought I had provided a great system and opportunity for staff. What I didn't realize was that while I had empowered those who presented, I left out every other person on staff. In fact, I had only slightly empowered those who presented because I gave them the topics. So I decided to do what I have heard is one of the things I do best. I asked for feedback from teachers beyond the surveys for the presenters. I truly wanted to know what worked and what needed to be changed. The demands rolled in, but not in the way a person would think. They spoke about the presenters not getting to see other sessions and wondered how I selected the topics or asked what we would be doing next. Two things became clear as I read the feedback. Teachers' support for their colleagues was rock solid and there was a feeling the experience could have been more beneficial for everyone. So I had to listen to the demands to get to the point where I freely empowered the teachers with what I did next.

I was excited as the survey answers came back. I had decided to completely open up the ability of any staff member to present at the next opportunity. What started out as me thinking I would have to get additional people, quickly became something where I couldn't fit everyone that had volunteered in the timeframe I had been given. So I decided to hold an in-house professional development conference that was put on and attended by our own staff! My job was to officially get out of the way and make sure the road was clear for anyone who wished to present. I designed a schedule that consisted of 3 sessions with 4 offerings each session. The offerings were wide ranging and selected by the teachers who were giving them[25]. Even more important was that, much like a conference, teachers attended the sessions they wanted; including the presenters when they weren't running a session. The teachers were completely empowered in what they presented and what they attended. It was a balance of empowerment that came about as a result of my letting teachers tell me what they wanted and how to improve. They had provided their own meaningful professional development.

We need to recognize two things that made this example of empowerment occur. First, go back to the first half of the story. Count how many times I used the word "I". I did it purposely to highlight a point, but in reality that word was at the forefront of my thinking. It was the Chris Jones show from start to finish. I created the schedule and assigned the topics and made sure teachers were at each workshop. It was an exercise of control under the illusion of empowerment. Second, look at the last half of the story. The teachers ran everything and I only gave them the time parameters in which they had to fit. It was a perfect example of what Matthew X. Joseph describes as "identifying the finish line and not the race."[26] This second format where teachers were given what they warmly demanded ended up far exceeding anyone's expectations of professional development. This was easy to hear as the discussions continued far after the sessions. Professional development will not look the same in our school because we trusted each other in both the process of ironing out struggles that came up and supported each other in the risk of taking a chance. This is not always an easy step.

Empowerment based on trust is a scary proposition for many leaders because they must accept and support the decisions made and actions taken by those they are empowering unless they are completely inappropriate for the situation at hand; Even if they are contrary to what the leaders would actually do themselves.

Even when there is the possibility of a person in a higher position disagreeing with the decision or action. Even in this type of situation it is crucial that the leader support the teacher who took the risk. When the empowerment of a teacher is properly supported it encourages that person and others who witness the act to continue taking chances and stretching to the end of their abilities in an attempt to grow. Furthermore, empowerment freely given and supported creates greater resilience among teachers. If we as leaders truly seek to break down the old hierarchy of positions and as a result change school institutions to learning communities, empowerment is the strongest tool.

Finally, in the end, empowerment is also about giving people the opportunity to add value to their current surroundings, improve by focusing on progress instead of perfection, and create a new story for themselves. Long lasting meaningful empowerment can be attained in any situation by building a culture of continuous improvement, leading with yes, and trust.

REFLECTION

People who consistently get results are often seen as high achievers and moved to leadership positions, but achievement is not always directly tied to the ability of the person who receives credit. How much of a role did controlling outcomes and getting near perfect results play in you becoming a leader in your current organization? What toll did that take on other areas of your life?

Empowerment is about creating an environment where educators are connected and creating value toward the whole through their personal agency and ability. What do you currently do in your leadership that explicitly shows educators you want this type of environment? How do you not just promote, but support, engage, and empower teachers in taking risks to grow?

ACTION STEPS

1. Select three people from your staff who you believe (or have shown you) are willing to take on some additional responsibility.

2. Give each of them control over a task (schedule, committee work, etc.) you usually do, but can spend your time doing something more productive due to your access and position.
3. Provide them with the big picture desired outcome, but not how they are supposed to accomplish it.
4. Do not step in to direct their progress. Just offer support as needed and accept their end result.
5. Reflect on the result with them and support their having taken the risk.
6. Repeat this with new staff members and give ownership of the tasks to those who have met some success.

VALUE ADDED

Much like the engagement piece of this book that states educators need to feel as if their personal story is recognized, accepted, and fits into the larger story of your organization, there is also a need for educators to feel more than just valued personally and professionally. For an educator to feel connected and act in a positive fashion with that agency they must see the value that they are able to add. This requires a clear connection to their values and an understanding of a unifying vision for the school and its students as a whole. If educators are to truly open themselves up to being empowered they must feel as if they add value to their current situation. It is imperative that leaders help make this happen by publicly acknowledging the value of those they serve on a consistent and authentic basis. This may sound blunt, but leaders who value their people empower them while leaders who devalue those they lead work to exercise tighter control over them. Even if that is not how you may feel, the message is clearly sent when you hold back on providing others the space to grow and improve. Sometimes, it is even seen as manipulative because the act of empowering is doing something for others while manipulation is getting others to do something for you. Once you empower people, everyone benefits.

I want you to really imagine what follows. Remember that person? You know that person. The one who is always being negative about others. They criticize everything about them. They insult their looks, how they talk, or what they like. If the person they are bent on tearing down has any success or is positive, the response is that they are lucky or even too stupid to realize they shouldn't be positive. I want you to really picture this person. Now imagine a time that they perform these behaviors to someone close to you like a sibling or even your child. Now I want you to picture the person being criticized coming to you upset about what's being said about them. Do you have it? Are you sitting in that emotion? What do you say when you realize it is up to you to comfort this person? Do you use the age old explanation that the person is just jealous? Or do you say they are just trying to tear the person down to make themselves feel better about all the areas in which they fall short? Personally, I use the latter. Which is why I transfer that explanation to not empowering teachers.

We must look within ourselves as leaders when we are controlling others to identify motivating factors. It is easy to say that there would be too many mistakes if we didn't, but mistakes are where real learning occurs; or at least that's what we tell our teachers and students to believe. Why don't we practice the same belief by releasing some control? It's true that there are some cases where we need to step in to make certain we get the required outcome (or as close as possible) the first time. After all, we are responsible for it being right.

> ### In the end however, much like the explanation we give to others, the need to control and not empower our teachers lies within the value we place on ourselves rather than them.

A much more straightforward way to state this is that, as leaders we need to fight off the imposter syndrome and mindset of scarcity if we are to truly empower others and grow as leaders. We only devalue others when we don't value ourselves. Think about how the value that we have for ourselves is directly related to how we act towards others. If we have a high value for ourselves we are able to live in humility and an acceptance of others being empowered. If not, we take the opportunity to devalue others to increase our value to ourselves. We do this through acts of control, doubt, or mistrust. That doesn't increase our value over all. Like the example earlier, it just gives us a temporary feeling of accomplishment. If you are clear on your areas of strength and how you add value as a leader it is much easier to release control to others which then raises their feeling of value. And everyone wants to feel as if what they have to offer adds value to the overall picture. It's one of the things that gets people through hard times and lends purpose to their day to day tasks. If we want to empower people we need to show them they are not just valued, but value added even when they fall short of our initial expectations. So how do we accomplish this?

It starts with a mindset and continues through purposeful actions towards showing those we lead that they are themselves capable of taking on the larger responsibility. Unfortunately, many teachers do not see themselves as leaders. Can you imagine that people who have so much impact on the lives of students, culture of the climate and building, and success of the school do not see themselves as a leader? This is often the result of outdated beliefs deeply rooted in the traditional understanding of leadership and its hierarchical structure. To break through that belief, teachers must not only be told, but shown that leadership comes in many forms void of a title or position. Once this is accomplished, those who follow you will do so because of the realization that they are fully capable and as a result add value. This is also a little on the selfish side for leaders. Today's leadership needs to be flexible and have the ability to accept responsibility for many areas. As a result, modern leaders don't need a group of individuals who wait to be directed in day to day actions, but instead an empowered group who take individual action toward the greater vision and become leaders themselves.

That means that teachers need to be involved in planning and developing school goals and the next steps required to fulfill the vision. Doing this has the three major lasting effects of increased responsibility, amplified voices, and positive culture. Allowing those who are looking to take on more responsibility the opportunity to step forward by automatically including them in the process sends the clear message that you are looking to empower people to take the lead in the designing of the organization's future success. It's important to realize that not all teachers are ready to step forward in an endeavor as large as school improvement. That doesn't mean that they are not capable. Involving everyone will provide you the chance to amplify the voices of some of the more quiet teachers. It will also serve to show them that they are capable and offer small opportunities to reinforce the value of their input. It is small steps like this that lead to increased participation and larger leadership roles in the future.

As discussed earlier, engaged teachers feel that connection to the larger vision. Including your staff in the process of creating the overall vision and steps needed gives them ownership and creates a positive atmosphere that assists in combating some of the negativity associated with any type of change. Additionally, many leaders struggle with consistent messaging around core values and plans for the future. Empowering staff to help craft that message automatically increases its consistency and frequency. If you are willing to be vulnerable as a leader and work horizontally rather than vertically with your staff by empowering them, you will notice that all of you will have a deeper understanding, better communication of, and greater focus on what is important and where to channel your energy.

Simply stated, but not simply accomplished, it's about providing opportunities, no matter how small, for input and leadership. Every building has individuals who are not living in their greatness. They show their ability to lead in the classroom and hallways, but often never realize their full potential. As a result they never have the impact they could possibly have on others. This happens for many reasons – both personal and professional – but can be reduced by a leader who focuses on empowering those they serve. Problems arise when the lack of empowerment is due to a leader's personal shortcomings or inability to make it happen. And we all know that every issue in a building is a leadership issue. The responsibility lies with us. Until we are ready to own that and adjust our mindset, we will struggle moving forward.

Finally, it's true that being empowered can feel both liberating and scary at the same time depending on the circumstance. Hesitation to start or take ownership for a project doesn't mean a person doesn't want to be empowered. It just means they need a different level of support moving forward. That is the responsibility of the leader. We must find that fine line between a feeling of being scared by the challenge or too scared to move forward and then exploit it for maximum benefit by supporting based on individual need. That means a leader must practice a balancing act between tight and loose control. This can be accomplished with a "yes and" approach. By using this, the leader creates a space where they are able to say yes to the teacher's idea, but create conditions for the change that helps ensure their own success. Repeating this behavior allows the leader to set fewer parameters based on the individual coming to them. The best part about this strategy is that it creates a culture of empowerment. I purposely used the word culture because it is deeper and longer lasting than climate. Once the leader models this behavior for and towards teachers it will most definitely become a mindset teachers own as they interact with students. After all, the end goal of empowering teachers is to build a world class educational environment for everyone

REFLECTION

Many people struggle with the imposter syndrome and often question the value they add to the larger group. What steps do you currently take as a leader to highlight the value that teachers in your building add to the improvement of what you do as a group? Now go deeper and think about what steps everyone else notices. Are you doing enough?

How many people are currently involved in and responsible for completing tasks connected to the overall goals of the school? Are you completing any tasks that can be given away as smaller leadership roles?

Those you serve need to feel connected to where they are going. They need to feel as if they are heard and their perspectives and opinions matter. How do you currently give voice at the leadership level to your teachers? Have you created strategies and systems to include even those who don't speak out?

ACTION STEPS

1. Assess your teachers' view of their value through a survey asking them to list both their personal and professional strengths.
2. Keep a record of how often you answer teachers with a "yes, but" rather than a "yes, and". Actively work to shift the balance week to week. If a written tally doesn't work for you try keeping 12 quarters in one of your pockets. Each time you answer a teacher with "yes, and" transfer one quarter to another pocket. Reward yourself with a coffee or tea using only the money you have transferred. Start with quarters and move to dimes as you get better.[27]

PROGRESS OVER PERFECTION

Another important set of words uttered by Fredrick Douglass on that day in 1857 are incredibly relevant to the ideas of just starting, not waiting for perfection, and accepting challenges as part of the process of progress were, "If there is no struggle, there is no progress."[28]

Another very important aspect of empowering those you work with is supporting and accepting progress over perfection as individuals grow into a new set of expectations and responsibilities. Doing this allows the focus to be more about the process and incremental progress of growth rather than the outcomes.

Success always appears within the iterations of new ideas put into practice.

All too often we as leaders fail to practice with teachers what we preach about students when it comes to failing forward and the phrase "not yet". Instead, we need to destigmatize the words failure and success by creating a mindset focused on the broader idea of consistent progression.

When you empower a teacher and set your expectation to the fact that they will receive value and become more engaged, the benefit is twofold. First, it becomes easier to move away from taking control by accepting the fact that they may not complete the task the way you would. However, that's where the idea of working the process, consistently moving toward success through multiple iterations, and the development of another person's ability comes into play. Second, those you serve in this manner gain confidence, take greater risks, and work harder because they are not focused on how they failed when they struggle or fall short. Instead the focus is on growth and development reached through the process of independence and empowerment.

Many institutions and classrooms like to hang up posters of Thomas Edison's words "I have not failed. I've just found 10,000 ways that won't work." While that is a great mindset, it lacks some of the constraints that we have as leaders when it comes to time and the servicing of students.

We don't have some of the luxuries required to faithfully apply that perspective to our very real situations. This is not to say that this thinking is wrong.

We just need to ask and then be willing to face the answer to the question; "What happens when this person fails." Asking that will help us as leaders separate the idea of short term situational failure from long term personal success.

Authentic empowerment has to occur over time through steps. It is a perfect example of growth through discomfort and for a leader to empower their people, it is necessary for them to experience and model existing in this realm.

Empowerment is often spoken about in terms of a person having the ability to make their own choices and as a result create outcomes of their design. This is true, but when done for personal or professional improvement, there must be uncertainty, vulnerability, struggle, and growth that occurs as part of the process. There are very few people who can just be empowered with large responsibilities on their first attempt. If that was the case, creating leaders would be an easy endeavor. Instead, I equate it to my childhood memory of blowing up a balloon. Take a moment to think of the last time you pulled a brand new balloon out of the bag. I always began pulling at it and stretching it with my hands with the idea of getting the balloon to inflate to the biggest size possible. I did this to make it easier to put more air into the balloon. Finally, I would blow it up, carefully judging the feeling of it accepting more air so I could stretch it to the maximum size. Have you ever done the same? Even better, have you done this and then let the air out only to blow it up again? I did it for one reason. It was always bigger the second time. To further illustrate the importance of gradual empowerment, I want you to think of the time you didn't stretch the balloon and kept inflating it to get it to the size you wanted only to have it suddenly pop under the strain.

Educators need to be continuously stretched in small increments and then celebrated for the successes that they have if there is to be long term empowerment. This stretching causes failure, but the mindset of reaching beyond your abilities, taking risks, and shouldering responsibility in the name of growth instead of outcomes will increase teachers' capacity for feedback and not personalizing falling short of the stated goal. This is the mindset leaders must model. One of the methods I use to do this are 15 minute meetings

Each January, at the halfway point in the school year, I meet with all of my staff for 15 minutes. Its size makes this difficult to get scheduled, but it is a priority. I use this time to model my need to continually improve what I am doing as well as receive feedback in an open accepting manner. I inform staff (the veterans already know this) that these meetings are about me and how I am doing. Yes, I want them to evaluate me. Our talk consists of them answering three questions. First, I ask them what I am currently doing that I need to immediately stop. In other words, what is bothering them about my day to day performance. These answers range from one time mistakes to those habits it takes others to point out. For example, a teacher told me she wanted to know more about course changes in her department. We had lost a teacher and as a result reassigned another teacher to take over an open class. The individual felt insulted that she was not offered the opportunity. She had always wanted to teach that class. An example of one of the everyday habits was the time a teacher told me she wished I would "increase my idle, more personal chatting so a better connection would be built." Next, I ask them what I am not currently doing that I need to start. This is my way of ascertaining where I am falling short. For example, there was a time where I needed to increase the amount of time I was spending in Special Education Classrooms. Having and acting on this information proved a powerful way to show my support. Finally, I ask them to give me one thing I can do to make their life easier or better. This is to show them I appreciate their honesty and that I hope to serve them better. Whether it is something as involved as advanced professional development around specific programs or tools or as simple as extra boxes of magnetic poetry for the classroom, I do whatever I can to honor any reasonable request. The whole process empowers them to advocate for their beliefs, illustrates that I will keep pushing forward, and highlights my need to iterate for long term success. It's important to realize that while the questions I ask are focused on how I need to improve to better serve, it never turns into a session based completely in negativity. That would be too much for anyone to handle. It has been my experience that the compliments and positive aspects of my leadership come pouring in at this time as well. Don't let these steer you from your mission of continually improving. Instead, save them in a "positive file" so you can look at them when you are feeling down and need a lift. Just because people don't always share compliments with you doesn't mean they are not thinking them. No one is perfect, but it helps to hear you are headed in the right direction. That only comes through authentic feedback.

This is one of the reasons the term "pilot" should be used much more often in schools. In fact, almost everything should be labeled a pilot until it has completed two to three iterations. Whenever there is a new pilot, people do not expect perfection. In fact, I would argue that they only expect limited success so that they can build something better on the part that didn't work. Pilots create what Daniel Coyle calls *ignition*[29]. *Ignition* is that burst of excitement and energy that people get with a new idea or initiative that resonates with them. This, when properly supported, creates momentum. Momentum is needed to push past obstacles, small failures and other constraints on the way to reaching the goal. Unfortunately, momentum only serves people for a certain amount of time. It ebbs and flows. To further illustrate my point, I always think and speak of a topic of conversation that came up while riding my bike on a sunny morning with my two boys.

We were on a particularly hilly course and getting a little tired near the end of the ride. As we were slowing down half way up a hill, I thought I would take the opportunity to share a life lesson.

I loudly announced: "We're almost there! We just have to push a little harder to get to the top. Just like any goal in life boys, we just had to work to achieve it" (the top of the hill in this case). "Now let's get after it!"

I was hoping to both motivate and teach like any overzealous dad would do. I thought I had hit the mark when my youngest called back to me. Yes, I was a little jealous that he wasn't breathing as hard as I was, but what he said gave me the energy to easily reach the top.

He yelled back. "Dad, the best part about getting to the top is that we get to coast down, but we can't enjoy that until we get to the top. Every up has a down. If we want to get to the good parts, we have to go through the bad parts."

As we crested the top and started to coast down the other side it wasn't long before another hill started to build in front of us, our momentum died down, and we had to begin pedaling again. This time though, we all had a renewed energy because we understood that the difficulty we were facing was temporary and we would again be rewarded just on the other side.

Momentum is powerful, but requires a rededication each time it slows to a halt because of an opposing force or constraint.

Ideally, leaders can influence the mindset of those they serve to view constraints as ways to unlock creative and ever changing solutions[30]. If this is accomplished, individuals will be motivated to embrace the ebb and flow of failure and success that is present whenever someone is working to be empowered. It is the leader's responsibility to make sure the person being empowered receives sufficient positive experiences to outweigh the negatives. This will sustain their motivation after momentum has subsided. Attaining success at any new endeavor requires the understanding of it being a process of progression rather than an arrival at perfection. Success is a process. Not a destination.

REFLECTION

All too often we see other people's success and wish we could do the same, feel as if we are not capable, get jealous, or label it as "lucky". No matter the feeling, it comes from an area of self doubt and misunderstanding. Success is the tip of the iceberg. The multiple steps and hard work is what lies beneath the water. The combination of these two emotions is a powerful block to progress.

1. What specific steps do you take as a leader to give others the confidence they need to be successfully empowered?
2. How do you change the perspective of those you serve so that they realize the goal of a task is to do it the best you can rather than the

best it has ever been done so a pathway to progress is created for future success?

3. What strategies do you have in place to help individuals retain their motivation when momentum fades?

ACTION STEPS

1. Select a few staff members (or even just one) who have expressed a desire to take on a little larger role in the building. Assign them each a task or project that has multiple steps, is complex, and has relatively low risk to them if it turns out poorly.

2. Provide the appropriate amount of structure concerning expected outcomes (broad), timeline, and resources.

3. Monitor the individual's progress in the event you need to provide appropriate advice or motivation.

4. Once they have finished, hold a conversation with these individuals during which you reflect on the positive accomplishments they had realized and what they struggled with while working on the task or project. Focus on the positives and how to address negatives moving forward.

5. Save your notes, reflect on what you should or could have done better, and begin to build a library of strategies to use with other people.

INSTRUCTION, PROFESSIONAL DEVELOPMENT, AND STORYTELLING

How do you get teachers to a point where they are empowered? By using ideal instruction, personalized professional development, and tremendous story telling. Let your teachers take risks, provide them the support to do this through learning opportunities that foster creativity, and then tell their story as if you were a reporter for the biggest story of your career. This cycle is at the heart of empowering your teachers. It provides them the space to stretch, supports them when they fall short, and shows everybody (including them) that such behavior is not only accepted, but encouraged by focusing on the positives of what they have just done. I have found that the mindset I have toward instruction assists me in this area. Being a teacher-centered leader means I focus on supporting, engaging, and empowering those I serve while still working toward my just cause by including everyone in the vision of an improved experience.

Part of this is not believing in what we like to call best practices that are the answer to everything in today's classrooms. Sure, as a whole there are research based practices, but I found through my doctoral research that in reality, there are only wise practices; nuanced and ever changing based on the students a teacher has at any given point. These wise practices are employed by teachers based on the current mood of the class, time of day, and context of the learning. Given this information, leaders need to empower teachers to take risks so that they may craft those wise practices day to day and class to class. Teachers need to have the confidence to understand and act on the times when a lesson plan has to be changed or thrown out at a moment's notice. Often our best learning comes from experiencing and adjusting to unplanned events. It takes a conscientious professional focused on knowing their students based on relationships they have built to employ wise practices in the classroom. In a culture void of empowerment, straying from the plan or doing something different is a practice for behind closed doors when administration isn't observing. This culture has to be stopped if teachers are ever to reach their highest level of success in serving students. Instead of being judgemental, leaders need to stay more open minded by leading with yes, observing practice, and saying "tell me more about what I just saw." These conversations are what will lead to reflection and adjustments to practice that will benefit students and build trust with the teacher. As a leader, the key to helping teachers create and use wise practices is to develop the mindset that there is no expert when it comes to wise practices. The only person who can make the best decision at the time is the one who knows the students best relationally and has the most experience in that specific environment. Leading with yes, observing, and helping teachers iterate will build confidence through trust and experience. This will empower teachers.

A teacher's ability to take risks and advantage of increased empowerment also requires relevant professional development. Providing this begins with the leader accepting responsibility for what options are made available for teachers to improve. I know there are the teachers who do not like attending professional development, but ultimately that is not because of them. That is because of me, the leader. You read that right. We cannot accept the thought that there are any teachers who do not want to improve their practice. It is the leader's responsibility to engage the teachers in professional development that is tailored to their specific needs. We do this by empowering them to self-select what they need to get better and the best format in which to learn. Doing so will give the teachers a sense of commitment, address their weaker areas, and make them an authority to others in areas of their choosing. Which, if you are still following the trail, will empower them to take risks and work with others. In fact, teachers can then use this to lead sessions of professional development for others.

I often think about ways in which I can empower teachers to increase their leadership capacity even before they leave the classroom for one main reason. I want them to understand the impact they have on not just their students, but the staff and overall building culture. When empowered to leverage that influence, teachers begin to better understand their actual value and ability to affect change. Giving teachers the opportunity to freely develop classes or departments and take risks in the classroom is a great model for everyone, but letting teachers take control of their own professional development is a higher level of empowerment. Ultimately, it gives them the ability to, as Nili Bartley says in her book by the same name, lead beyond their title and create change.[31] This is easier said than done.

I struggled with giving complete control to the teachers until I solicited, truly listened to, and implemented ideas from feedback. Reflecting on what I was being told gave me an important message that we often miss as leaders. Teachers wanted control over their own learning so they could personalize it to their needs.

It was up to me as a teacher-centered leader to provide them the structure that allowed their learning to occur rather than making them fit their learning into a familiar format.

Reflecting on my personal journey to get to that point, I found I had unwittingly followed three phases which I now refer to as easy, medium, and hard to get to a place where I stepped away and fully empowered teachers.

The easiest way to begin empowering teachers you have in your own building to run professional development is by giving up time in your meetings. We all have faculty, department, and planning meetings that can use some revamping. You only give up a little control, but this is a good starting point for those teachers who may not be ready to completely take over. Take an idea, strategy, or tool that will be helpful for your staff and have a teacher spend 15 minutes speaking about it at a staff meeting. Do the same for 30 minutes of a department meeting. Try combining groups during department or planning meetings. Have teachers in those smaller groups lead mini workshops on strategies they all use. For example, I had two teachers explain the benefits of mindful minutes and then lead the staff in one at the beginning of a faculty meeting. I also had the Social Studies and English Departments meet as a group where they were led (by teachers) in a workshop on the Notice and Note Strategy so they could use it with non-fiction and create a common language among students when accessing texts. Both of these were demonstrations that left the teachers with strategies to take back to their own classes. The most valuable takeaway was that teachers were the ones who provided the new strategies. While this worked and was a step away from controlling and a step closer to empowering, I had still selected the topics and teachers. I needed to branch out and ask teachers who were a little quieter to step forward. So I decided to move to what I now call the medium level of difficulty and take on an early release professional development day.

This next level of difficulty when empowering your teachers through professional development is accomplished by having them run sessions on an early release or even full professional development day at your school. You start this process by researching what your staff needs. This is done through a combination of meeting with them, looking through walkthrough data, and checking in on their goals. Put the answers to this information together with licensure requirements and then tap into the teachers who have expertise. Make sure you look for those who may be a little shy about leading a session and support them in taking the step forward. For example, my state requires 15 professional development points in both special education and sheltered English immersion training. I tapped teachers to lead hour-long sessions on instructional strategies for special education, English language learners, and Google Classroom. I then split the staff into three groups and rotated them through each session. Everyone got the points they needed and strategies they could put to use. I also had teachers complete evaluations. These evaluations were key in three areas. They gave support and reassurance to the presenters, provided proof to award professional development points to the attendees, and gave me feedback on how to improve moving forward. This feedback was critical in my taking the next step, the hardest, and fully empowering my staff in this area.

The most difficult, both physically and mentally, but most exciting and beneficial way for leaders to fully empower their teachers in the area of professional development is to hold an in-house conference put on and attended by your teachers. Ask your staff for volunteers by informing them you are looking for people to present some of the standout practices or initiatives they are currently using and pursuing to their colleagues. Suddenly, you have a diverse set of practices being shared, learned, and better understood by teachers; for teachers. For example, my teachers volunteered to run workshops ranging from the importance of movement[32] to gamification and utilizing a deskless classroom[33] to strategies for accessing text[34] to debating homework[35] to name just a few! These were topics I would have never picked as the leader of a building. I was overwhelmed by the amount of volunteers I had and wanted to honor all of them for having volunteered. Working with my assistant principal David Floeck, who is much better at designing schedules than me, a conference style schedule was created and teachers went to the presentations in which they were interested. Not one was empty. The added benefit above their choice and volunteering to present was that the presenters were able to attend sessions as well.

The idea of taking the lead is not always an easy thing to bring to fruition. Sure, teachers may get there after some time with leading professional development sessions, but there are multiple things they do in our buildings each day that show leadership and have an impact. It's our responsibility to notice as many of those as possible and make room for more and greater iterations. Many individuals like freedom, but shy away from too much of it because of the responsibility aspect. The idea of owning the outcome often causes a twinge of fear or the rise of imposter syndrome. Some are scared about what success or failure will personally mean to them and as a result may need a nudge away from the same routine that provides a feeling of safety. Again, that is our responsibility as leaders to nudge them into greater success.

I truly believe it is always better to be nudged forward by choice before being dragged forward by initiative or regulation.

To combat this hesitancy, leaders need to publicly build up and increase the relevance of those who are making attempts. Doing this builds their confidence, but also creates an urge in others to join in the push to be empowered. This is why it's incredibly important to publicize their successes every chance you get.

Simply put, leaders need to become master storytellers on multiple platforms so they are able to publicize their teachers like they are the biggest lead on the nightly news. My definition of master storyteller is quite simple. Take to all forms of media and put evidence of what is occurring out to the world. It doesn't have to be in a perfect format. It just has to get out there where everyone gets to see it. There will be detractors, but that is ok. Trust me when I say do not respond to them. Just keep to your positive message about what your teachers are doing. Whenever there is a teacher who is taking risks, collaborating with colleagues, leading professional development, or showing they are empowered in any other way, the leader has to take to social media and brag about them. However, this is where I offer a note of caution and test whether or not you have taken the time to get to know those you serve.

I always say that everyone loves to be patted on the back for a job well done. That is true, but not everyone likes it in a large public manner. Some teachers are purposefully very passive participants on different forms of social media.

It is not for a leader to judge a person for how they like to be recognized, but instead recognize them in a way that has the desired effect of support and continued empowerment.

This is not to say that leaders should slow down with promoting on social media. In fact, doing so in a broad way that allows other people (especially colleagues) to add to the compliments empowers the highlighted teacher to continue doing the same things. What about the other teacher who doesn't want to be recognized on social media? That's ok because they still see it and are supported, engaged, and empowered to continue because the leader is bragging about their same type of behavior or performance. Just make sure you find a way to let them know they are seen just as much as the person on social media. Teachers have an incredibly difficult job. It is essential for principals to make those they serve feel as if they are seen, appreciated, and valued beyond a number on a roster that watches students in a room. Personalization of recognition and the use of social media helps accomplish this. A strong sense of support for their risk taking, collaboration, and growing leadership as well as the empowerment to continue.

One last word about continuing. I mentioned the negative aspects of some individuals on social media. It would be disingenuous for me to ignore the fact that they are out there. I challenge leaders to seek out these pockets of negativity and flood them with the positive aspects of what your teachers are doing for two simple reasons. First, teachers will realize that you support what they are doing and empower them to continue. Second, narratives are built by being vocalized, challenged, or proven. You do not have to respond to negative comments. In fact, ignore them. Once you build up a narrative of positivity, other individuals will start to handle the negative people for you. I say trust me because I have used this technique and found success. Think about this for a minute. Ideas are nothing without action. Leaders often sit with other people in education and complain about the negative things people say about us without having the knowledge about what actually occurs in schools.

It is ultimately our responsibility as leaders to tell the real story of the great things teachers are doing and what's occurring in our schools each day.

Telling them will drown out the negative and allow the positive to spread. Think about the fact that if you are not telling the story or creating the narrative, someone else is. As a leader, why would you ever let anyone else tell the story of your school?

REFLECTION

Do a majority of your teachers take risks in the classroom? Are they open to this or too worried that it will look bad on their evaluation? What do you currently do to encourage instructional risk taking in your teachers? How can you improve this?

What does your current model of professional development for staff look like? Is it individualized? Do your teachers have a choice among a variety of relevant offerings? How can you improve what you currently do by empowering the teachers in your own building?

What is the story of your school? Are you currently sharing everything occurring in your school with the community at large? How can you increase the amount of positive reinforcement and recognition your teachers receive?

Have you modeled taking risks, failing, and iterating for improvement for your teachers?

ACTION STEPS

1. Get into classrooms every day and just observe what some of your more progressive teachers are doing.
2. Leave them some positive feedback on a tool like Voxer and include a question that shows you support taking risks.
3. Revisit their classrooms and appropriately publicly praise (social media, faculty meeting, etc.) them for taking a chance by doing something different or new.
4. Analyze your current system of professional development.
5. Discover your staff's abilities to provide and areas of need (conversations, surveys, etc) as soon as possible.
6. Begin the process of empowering your staff to take control of their professional development by following the easy, medium, and hard levels of difficulty.

EMPOWERMENT CHALLENGE

Empowering others is difficult because it often requires leaders to change their way of thinking. It is about being able to step away from a specific responsibility by giving it to someone else and accepting their product as a step in the process of empowerment rather than a destination marked as a success or failure. Sure the accountability still lies with the leader, which makes it even more difficult to give up control, but the ultimate goal of empowerment is to create a capacity to lead in others. None of this can happen without intention.

1. Do you take the time to plan how you are going to support risk taking in the classroom, provide individualized professional development, and tell the story of those teachers responding
2. How much value do your teachers feel they have and what are you currently doing to increase that level?
3. What are you going to do to show your teachers that they are part of the school vision and have a responsibility to work toward its fulfillment by taking leadership roles?

This is all possible to accomplish by focusing on every step toward change being just that, a step toward the ultimate goal as long as teachers are being increasingly empowered. Start thinking about areas where you are involved, but not empowering others and then take that step away. The first is the hardest because you won't realize how ready your teachers are until they show you themselves. You will not be disappointed.

WISE PRACTICES AND TOOLS

LEADERSHIP OPPORTUNITIES: One of the best ways to empower teachers is to provide them with opportunities to lead. This can be done by placing them in charge of effective committees. By effective I mean ones that have visible, meaningful outcomes and further connect teachers to the overall vision and mission of the school. You can still be a sitting member, but let your teachers run the School Improvement Committee, Culture Committee, or Handbook Committee. When you use committees in this fashion make sure you take the opportunity to coach them along the way, but do not get actively involved in the process beyond clearing obstacles. It is also essential that you support the outcome of the teachers' leadership opportunity, but reflect in a positive way on possible improvements.

PROMOTION: Make use of social media beyond the regular tweet or post. Research various, easy to use tools such as WeVideo and Animoto for videos and Smore for newsletters. Put your pictures together and create short videos about what is occurring in your school. This automatically creates multiple postings and keeps the good works of your school in the public eye. Create a main school hashtag and then others for different programs[36]. This will also help you collect every post and further publicize people. You should be sending a weekly newsletter on a consistent basis to build expectations. Put pictures, videos, and shoutouts in, but more importantly have your teachers contribute material. They can give updates and other pieces of writing that go out to the community. Let them know that you will not be changing what they give you and then follow through. They, before you, need to be the ones that are proud of what people are seeing.

CYCLE OF CONTINUOUS IMPROVEMENT: Build this mindset by putting structures in place that encourage people to identify challenges, share successes, attempt new things, and then reflect collaboratively on how to improve. This is particularly effective if you take a baseline of something a teacher is doing, work the process laid out in this section, and then return to them with a glimpse of their old level of performance. This validates their efforts and begins to solidify the continuous improvement mindset. Make sure to not focus on getting better because they are lacking, but instead because of how much better they could be with just a one percent increase.

STAFF MEETINGS: Have teachers contribute to the material for staff meetings. Once they start doing this, give over time for them to run portions of the meetings. Have them take turns individually or as departments sharing instructional strategies or innovative practices. Model your willingness to support risk taking or out of the box thinking by supporting teachers taking visible leadership roles in areas historically reserved for the principal. Personally, I consider it a successful staff meeting if there are shout outs, a learning portion, and I don't run the whole meeting. I try to give control of the meeting to two to three people each month by informing them as early as possible so they can prepare and feel comfortable.

PROFESSIONAL DEVELOPMENT: Use the easy, medium, and hard levels of professional development discussed earlier in this section. Start with small steps to assess how many risk takers are willing to step forward. Engage your teachers to discover what they really need as departments or individuals. People know what they need help with. The issue is creating a culture in which they feel comfortable sharing that information. Once they start and you empower, a few others will follow. This will increase the amount of those who feel empowered to contribute. Teachers will soon be seen as leaders by their colleagues and as a result will become leaders in action.

TRAIN THE TRAINER: A lot of leaders sign on to the idea of a train the trainer model for many different programs, but few actually get to a meaningful application. This model is a great way to make use of department meetings, common planning time, or any other time you have set aside in your schedule. These make for a great first step of empowering a teacher to come forward and lead because it is a small setting and usually among their close colleagues. Another bonus is that you don't have to wait to send the teachers for an official training on a topic. As the leader, there are many areas in which you can offer to train a teacher and then have them present to others. This method saves time and keeps a unified message concerning whatever is being taught.

ONE LAST THING...THAT MAYBE SHOULD HAVE BEEN MENTIONED EARLIER

Sgt. Major Mulcahy: "The boy is your friend, is he?"
Col.Shaw: "We grew up together, yes."
Sgt. Major Mulcahy: "Let him grow up some more."
Col. Shaw: "I see."

This dialogue between a drill instructor and his officer concerning the men they are preparing taken from the movie Glory is significant in many ways[37], but for the purposes of supporting, engaging, and empowering your teachers it gives rise to a word I had been considering for this circle, but did not include. It highlights the importance of being able to step away even when those you ultimately serve are struggling. It is uncomfortable to watch someone stretch and struggle, but essential if they are going to successfully grow. The reward ultimately comes at the end of the journey if the proper process is followed. This process requires support and engagement, but also a diminishing amount of involvement.

The word involvement signifies an often overlooked, but really important nuance in moving from engaged to empowered. It is the highest form of engagement when looking at the person engaged and the lowest form of empowerment from the viewpoint of the person who is trying to empower others. It signifies the gradual release of control over circumstances, actions, and outcomes. While at first glance that sounds confusing because it is from two different perspectives, consider the following: When someone is engaged at the lowest level they are paying attention. They realize what's occurring and are following along. The shift to being involved comes after the highest level of engagement. That is when the person is excited about what's going on and wants to be part of it. Once they fully step into the action and start owning the outcomes, they are involved. I consider involvement as the highest level of engagement because it is the actual act of creating and molding whatever is occuring. A teacher who is involved is getting their hands a little dirty in the process. For example, a parent is engaged when they are constantly checking their student's grades and setting a structure for them to complete work at home. A teacher is engaged when they contribute to a positive culture or work in accordance with the leader's agenda. A parent is involved when they are not just staying current with what is happening, but helping their student at home with techniques and strategies. A teacher has become involved when they are not just contributing to the culture, but actively and consciously bringing others along.

The same framework applies to leaders. Engaged leaders regularly go into classrooms, but they take that time to check off boxes and make sure the curriculum is being covered. An involved leader is actually getting involved in the lessons and giving authentic, meaningful feedback. This nuance highlights the mental bridge a leader needs to cross to truly empower their teachers.

You have to be involved as a leader to offer support to your teachers, but you can't stay too involved as they become increasingly engaged. Especially if you are looking to empower them.

The key to empowerment is actually stepping away from being so involved so that the person can do something on their own. This is the trap of involvement. It feels good so we want to keep doing it and often don't realize that everyone can achieve more if we gradually involve ourselves to stimulate independence and growth. Remember that kid whose parents were helping practice at home? Eventually, that kid has to do that on their own because the parent will not be on the stage or field with them when they need to perform. How about that teacher who can take an instructional risk that you have pre-approved and talked about, but then is expected to face a new situation without you knowing or being there ahead of time? Unless they are empowered to try new things on their own they will not grow as much as they can. When working with teachers it's important to be involved as they try new strategies or lessons in the classroom, but eventually they need to do so without your guiding presence. A leader can have an engaged teacher, show them ways to be empowered, and even be involved during the first attempt by offering tips, tricks, and even a lifeline if needed, but eventually that leader needs to step away to truly empower that individual.

Stepping away from someone as they carve their own path is never an easy thing to do. The chance of failure will always be present. Often, because you are the leader, that failure will reflect on you. What you need to recognize as a leader is that there are many times, with the proper support, that we all need to "grow up some more." It takes trust and a firm grip on the knowledge that it is truly the only way a person can reach their full potential to successfully empower people on a consistent basis. When it comes to empowerment; know it, feel it, and do it. The results will amaze you.

VIGNETTE

I was tired of hearing about summer reading being a drag. Classes assigned reading and advanced placement courses had reading on top of that. I thought about how all of those students had summer reading assigned, but the other students in the academic classes didn't really have much to read. What bothered me even more than that was the idea that students would come back to school to a test about what they had read. Not only was this assigning negative feelings to the thought of reading, but also drove it home when a student would start their new year with zeros or some other form of an "F". Welcome back (sarcasm intended)! These reasons are why I was a huge supporter of the Summer Read Smackdown![38]

This event was specifically designed to elicit student voice in the choice for a whole school summer read. I knew it had worked at my previous school due to the hard work of Suzanne Larson, our Library/Media Specialist. I added to this process by declaring the first two days of school Interdisciplinary Days[39] during which teachers would take something from the summer read that was related to their area of study and teach a little more in-depth about it for the sake of learning instead of grading whether or not the students had read. The effect was two-fold. First, students would not start the year with poor grades. Second, the activities in classes encouraged students who had not read the book yet, to continue reading. I decided it was something we had to try at this new, much larger school.[40]

I wasn't sure how it would turn out. I had mentioned the idea of a "Summer Read Smackdown" activity as a way to increase student interest in reading by giving them a voice in choosing an all school summer read to the English Curriculum Coordinator. She then brought it to her department and explained the process and reasoning with excitement in her voice. Before I realized they were moving forward with trying this, one of the English teachers created a teaser video. I helped spread the video all over social media and checked in on the process being led by the coordinator. She informed me that the librarian was running the process with her as well. Selections started coming into the library, and students were given a little direction about how to defend their book in public. Then we held the event that had teachers running a tournament of books being argued for by students in a library packed with 200 kids watching and voting.

We publicized the event and were then invited to speak at the State House explaining what we had done. Beyond this, the student who argued for the winning book ended up landing an internship with a State Representative at the State House. My head was spinning. All I had done was make a connection between our Librarian, English Curriculum Coordinator, and my previous Library/Media Specialist and then step to the side. I supported where I could and bragged all over social media. The three of them took it to the next level. I have always believed in empowering teachers, who then will empower their students, but this was something beyond what I had ever imagined would happen. I have been a teacher-centered principal for years, but what I witnessed cemented the belief that all leaders need to embrace and live if they want to be as effective as possible.

Trust teachers, let them go, and be amazed!

REFLECT ON EMPOWERMENT

"I never lose. I either win or learn." – Nelson Mandela

That time I stood in front of the professor with a pit in my stomach gently reminding me that there will be those who do not feel it as well as those who do when faced with being empowered is something that has stayed with me to this day. The idea of looking at someone and telling them they shouldn't be asking if what they have done is good enough, but instead giving it to you and saying this is the best I could do. Years of societal programming has made that incredibly difficult for many. I hated that feeling and yet here I am writing about taking that chance with others. It may sound a little hypocritical, but it's only so if you approach the act of empowering others without offering any kind of support or engagement. Not to mention clear communication around requirements and being involved to a certain level.

I came to focus on making this easier for others by reflecting on a classroom walkthrough practice I employ. I always ask students three questions whenever I visit a classroom. I ask if they know what they are learning? It's important for them to be able to articulate the concept or fact on which they are focusing during the lesson. I then ask students how they know when they understand it? This question alone usually shows whether or not they understand the concept through their explanation to me. I finish by asking how they will show the teacher they understand? This usually gets either a good response or they fall back to something similar to "on a test." I am sure you can imagine how happy students are to see me come over to their desk during class!

In all seriousness, it is my expectation that students can answer these questions. That said, if that is my expectation of teachers to be able to have students answer those questions, then I must also fulfill the expectation that teachers will be able to answer those questions when asked about being empowered. Otherwise I am only creating that bad feeling in the pit of a teacher's stomach when I push to have them take risks or begin to lead. Leaders must have clear communication about their expectations. Doing so will not only provide a sense of support, but also serve to engage teachers in the process of empowerment and growth.

One of the worst phrases I can hear as a leader is "what do you want me to do?" That means they're just being a good person or teacher and are not really that engaged. The goal for leaders if they are truly empowering their staff is to have people come to them with suggestions on how to improve, new perspectives, or different ideas they have. This takes a specific culture in your building that encourages the growth of leadership. Stop reading right now, take out something to write with and on, and answer the following questions:

1. How are you currently implicitly and explicitly empowering your teachers?
2. How do teachers know when they have been empowered?
3. What are your teachers doing with that empowerment?

KEY TAKEAWAY

If empowerment is the transfer of power from those who traditionally hold it as a mantle of their position to those who may deserve to hold it for their experiences, creativity, or as an answer to their systemically expected silence; it is going to take a new kind of leader to enact it successfully. When focusing on empowering others, leaders must adopt the behaviors of uncovering and creating connectivity while highlighting its value. This takes a dogged determination to discover the "why", core values, or motivation of those you serve. They will not often volunteer these aspects of their personality until you have built up the relationship and trust needed for them to be uncovered. The authentic empowerment of those individuals who take a chance stepping forward must start with a new mindset for many leaders. How often does that voice within say that we are the best suited to complete a task? We often find ourselves overloaded with responsibility because our inner dialogue instructs us that it is just easier for us to do the job instead of teaching someone else. The mindset of progress over perfection is essential if we are to move away from the culture crushing belief that every outcome has to be perfect or done exactly the way we want the first time. After all, don't we tell our teachers to embrace student creativity and treat times they fall short of the mark as learning opportunities? The same principle applies to those we lead. We all just have to communicate that it's what we believe. If we carry this belief in our hearts, it becomes easy to act on empowering and praising teachers in the areas of instruction, professional development, and storytelling.

ENDNOTES

[24] This was originally said in a speech Fredrick Douglass gave at Canandaigua, New York, on August 3, 1857, the twenty-third anniversary of the West India Emancipation. They began with the words, "If there is no struggle, there is no progress."

[25] The titles of some of the sessions were: Researching Vaping and Possible Solutions, Notice and Note: Now What?, Tools for Access: Modifying Content for English Learners, Hidden Benefits: Why Movement is as Important as Academics, Making Homework Meaningful, and Student Engagement...Give Me a Break!

[26] SEEing to Lead podcast episode 19 "Start With the Big Picture and Then Support"

[27] I first learned of this technique in the Guiding Principals cohort of Daniel Bauer's Mastermind.

[28] These words began a section of Fredrick Douglass' speech at Canandaigua, New York, on August 3, 1857, the twenty-third anniversary of the West India Emancipation where he spoke about conceding power.

[29] The Talent Code: Greatness isn't born. It's grown. Here's how. Random House (Daniel Coyle, 2009)

[30] Daniel Bauer talks about "Beautiful Constraints" in his School Leadership Series podcast episode by that title dated 7/17/2019. This concept is explained in detail in the book A Beautiful Constraint: How To Transform Your Limitations Into Advantages, and Why It's Everyone's Business written by Marc Barden and Adam Morgan and published by Wiley in 2015.

[31] Lead beyond Your Title: Creating Change in School from Any Role. Dave Burgess Consulting Incorporated, 2019

[32] The workshop Hidden Benefits: Why Movement is as Important as Academics was given by Russell Nolan, Lexi Watkins, Heidi Martin, and Lori Medeiros

[33] The workshop Student Engagement...Give Me a Break! was given by Amanda Ferrara and Amanda Reagan

[34] The workshop Notice and Note: Now What? was given by Amy Floeck

[35] The workshop Making Homework Meaningful was given by Deborah Caruso

[36] Our main hashtag is #WHPantherPride. We also have #WHPantherPathways for our college and career readiness programming. Another hashtag is #WHArtsMatter to highlight any events, awards, or work going on with art.

[37] Glory, TriStar Pictures(1989)

[38] There are many summer read or monthly tournaments of books, but the Summer Read Smackdown was an idea first implemented (at least as far as the model I used and have expanded) by Suzanne Larson, the Library/Media Specialist who was at Seekonk High School in Seekonk, Massachusetts at the time of its inception.

[39] This term and idea came from multiple discussions with Brian McCann, the principal of Case High School in Swansea, Massachusetts.

[40] My current school has a population twice the size of the previous school that this initiative was started.

CONCLUSION

It was a hot Saturday afternoon. All of us standing in that huddle, looking at each other with sweat and dirt streaked faces, uniforms, and bodies that were tired. We had been playing as hard as we could, but the team we were up against was clearly our equal if not even a little better. Our morale was already strained and there was a good chance it was about to break. We stared down the field at the first down marker we needed to get to if we wanted to stay in the game. One of us asked, "What is it? How far do we need to get?" The reply came with a disgusted tone, "50 yards. It's first and 50." The groans were audible and our body language was most likely even louder. The referees finished marking off the yardage and as the action was ready to start once again, we resigned ourselves to running a few plays and heading back to the sideline. That's when the whistle blew and we saw our coach had called a time out.

You may be asking how we got into such a bad yardage situation so let me lend some context. We ran our first play (off tackle) of the series and broke our running back for a 60 yard gain. The problem was that one of the referees called holding (10 yard penalty) on a player that wasn't anywhere near the action. Our coach didn't care for that and decided to let the referee know his displeasure. It was only a brief period of time before the referee decided to inform our coach that he didn't like being questioned in that manner by throwing a yellow flag high in the air for unsportsmanlike conduct (15 yard penalty), which only served to encourage my coach to further question why the referee would throw a flag on him for disagreeing with a bad call. That was the first day I learned that referees, at least this one did, carry two flags and really don't have a problem using them. The second flag for unsportsmanlike conduct

(15 yard penalty) stopped the conversation on the sideline as we were wondering what just happened.

We could only imagine what he was going to say when he got out to the huddle, but we never could have imagined the reality of what actually happened. He stepped in the middle of the huddle, took his hat off, rubbed his head, and did something that has made me strive to be a leader like him. He looked at each one of us, apologized for putting us in that position and explained that while the excitement had gotten the best of him, he was wrong and never expected us to act that way. Our coach then asked us for a favor. We couldn't believe he was asking us to help him! The exact words of the speech he gave us are not for this book, but as he patted us on the head and put his arm around us he gave us the belief we could make that 50 yards. This is just one example of the many from my high school football coach, Tom Ryan, that show he practiced SEEing others and increasing the rotation of the circle to perfection.

In this one instance, he saw from the sideline we were breaking so he stopped the action to give us a breather and collect ourselves. Knowing we would need support to do this, he came out, accepted his responsibility for the situation, and worked with us mentally to re-engage us in the work we needed to do. Coach could have stopped there; letting the scene play out and put it on us. He didn't. He took the next step and empowered us to find our own way to success. You may ask how that empowerment looked. Coach Ryan told us we could call our own plays. He told us he was the one asking us to get out of the situation he put us in and as a result wouldn't blame us if we couldn't. He only asked for our best effort. He made it low risk and low pressure. Sometimes it takes a hard situation to force us into trying something different or taking a risk. Many times that risk pays off because the sense of urgency and ownership has not only been increased, but accepted.

We made the 50 yards and the first down, but we still lost the game. Ultimately, we won because in that moment, when we faced loss, we had experienced something we could take forward with us to any new struggle we faced. The idea that we had it within ourselves to ultimately succeed in the face of failures along the way. We had been supported, engaged, and empowered in a lasting way.

I am often reminded by this story and those young men who experienced it with me that it took years (for me at least) to understand, verbalize, and pass on to others what had occurred. Much like this, it's hard to see the future outcomes in education because it takes years of changing thought patterns rather than building projects. The people leaders serve are individuals and as a result require different supports to become engaged or empowered.

> **Leaders must come to not just realize, but fully understand that people experience their environment through the culture in which they exist, because water, or in this case people, seeks its own level.**

A negative culture breeds mistrust, a lack of belonging and understood value, and an outcome focused environment. A positive culture on the other hand focuses on coaching, clear messaging around how to continuously improve, connection, risk-taking, and progress over perfection. We all have choices about what type of environment we foster. The question becomes what am I, as a leader, doing to build authentic relationships through support, engagement, and empowerment outside my personal comfort zone and inside others' personal culture. What does that question look like for you? Even better, what does the answer look like?

For me, it begins with a mindset. I believe that if the teachers are supported in improving their practice, engaged in moving toward their passion and/or purpose, and then empowered to live in that area; it becomes a situation where everyone wins because we are all on the same "side". All too often conversations arise that are centered on "them" and "us". As a leader, I would love to say this is just what teachers do, but I would be dishonest if I were to say the same conversations didn't happen around the leadership table. That is where I work to both internalize and vocalize that everyone is doing the best they can. The only "side" in education that matters is the students; with the ultimate goal of preparing them all for the world of opportunities that awaits if they are willing to grab it. This whole concept of supporting, engaging, and empowering teachers is about leveraging existing resources to that end. It's about leaders finding the way to maximize their impact on students. I have found that supporting, engaging, and empowering the teachers in your buildings is the best way to make the biggest splash in the lake of student lives and success.

Let's face it. Nobody ever got into teaching or leadership to suck. We all chose to make a difference in people's lives. Both teachers and leaders exercise that ability to choose every day. Clearly we don't decide if we are going to show up or change careers each day, but we definitely choose how we will show up or continue our career. Think about who in this equation has a very limited choice over how much they enjoy and excel at what they are doing. You couldn't be more right if your first thought was about the students. Just like the students' choice of how they "show up" or bring themselves to the experience of school; it is also the teachers' and leaders'. It isn't difficult to understand that while a persons' attitude is ultimately up to them, it is influenced by how they are treated in various situations. That is why it is the leader's responsibility to make sure teachers are supported both personally and professionally so that they have the ability to improve their positive impact on students. Achieving that directly affects more students than any leader working on their own regardless of their skill set or level.

This cycle is about leaders acting on their responsibility to engage teachers in the process of continually improving. By consistently supporting, engaging, and empowering teachers, leaders close a continuous loop. This creates a better culture and builds leaders among the teaching staff who in turn begin to practice the "loop" on other teachers and more importantly, students. This type of culture is far deeper than an immediate climate change and takes time to develop. Almost every interaction I have with a teacher is done with an eye towards developing a deeper and more trusting relationship. I do this by opting for face to face meetings over email, having difficult, respectful conversations to address "elephants in the room", and providing multiple opportunities for teachers to take the lead on what works best for them to continually improve. If I support, engage, and empower my teachers to the point that they don't just have to come into work, but are motivated to; there is no way the students do not experience a higher opportunity for success. Isn't that the "side" we are all on? What would you have to do to get the majority of your staff to like coming to work? If you haven't thought or acted on that, what are you waiting for to start? Teaching can be a grind. Teachers lose that hop in their step concerning their work all the time until they either reimagine what they are doing or someone helps them rediscover the beauty of this profession. Be the leader who does that for them. You have the power to make that difference. Many times, as I have discussed, it just takes the sometimes difficult task of successfully reframing the situation to accomplish.

Like many other aspects of life, the more you practice reframing the better you get. Additionally, once you become more proficient, others are influenced when they hear the positive stories you help them tell themselves. Reframing isn't a one time occurrence. You don't say a few positive things to yourself and then suddenly escape negative self-talk. Especially if you are used to being negative or find yourself easily influenced by it. This whole book has mentioned strategies and concepts that show how reframing is a powerful tool that helps the whole process by increasing the speed of the circle. It is up to the leader to know their people enough so they can step in and offer support by engaging and empowering them in the process of reframing their story.

For example, when a teacher falls short of expectations or does something wrong, you need to support them. They are already living in the fact that they've fallen down. As their leader, you need to reframe that thought and feeling of failure by pointing out that they've made a small step towards positive change and getting better. It isn't about not being honest, but instead focusing on the positive progress they have made as a way to encourage them to work with you in creating a plan for them to get better.

When someone you serve is not engaged, the reframing has to occur with you. As a leader you must look at what you can do better to engage them. It is far too easy for leaders to say that people aren't interested and nothing they do will matter. That is the type of negative talk that keeps things from moving forward. Think about the last time you were not engaged in an activity. Was it the activity itself or the planning? Maybe your group make-up needed a different activity. Maybe the planning was lacking. Could it have been the timing or delivery? All of those are leadership issues. Teachers don't get engaged for faculty meetings that are at the end of a long day and consist of being talked at for an hour. Many of us know this, but we continue to do it. Teachers are not going to engage in trying new instructional strategies, work harder to not have their effort recognized, or look to help make positive changes if they do not feel supported. They are not lazy or do not care. Stop and reframe it for a moment. What if they feel undervalued and are asking "what's the point?" That's a leadership issue. Finally:

When you are trying to empower people as a leader you need to reframe your thinking from how you traditionally look at being empowered to how those who are receiving the opportunity to be empowered feel.

If giving someone the opportunity to be empowered comes with "strings attached", strict constraints, or doesn't address the progress over perfection piece by highlighting the value added; it will just become another task on their list of responsibilities that you don't want to do. That's why leaders need to help those they are looking to empower by providing support through resources and planning, connecting it to their personal vision, and praising the progress they have made before another, better, stronger iteration.

That repeated and improved empowerment is what will make the difference. Think about the first time you were a leader of any type. Remember when you brought that first project, idea, or decision to fruition? Reflect on it. Sure it wasn't perfect, but it was yours. Dig deep and feel that feeling again. Why would we not want every person in our care to feel that sense of accomplishment, satisfaction, and confidence? Because that is what made us do it again and again until we got to where we are now.

There is a story of an old Rabbi[41] that highlights one of the underlying drivers for leaders to empower those they lead and help them succeed beyond their own expectations. Coupled with the overall objective of supporting, engaging, and empowering teachers as a way to leverage a more positive culture and school experience that results in high student and teacher success far beyond a leader's capacity to attain were it done individually or in solitude, the story points to lasting impact rather than momentary gains.

There was a very wise Rabbi who was quite famous living in Europe. Because of his wisdom and fame there was a man living in the United States that wanted to visit him. So this man travels all the way to the Rabbi's place in Europe. When he gets there, he finds a beautiful, ornately decorated house. The visitor is immediately greeted at the door and treated with a tremendous amount of respect. Once he is brought to the Rabbi's living quarters, the visitor is shocked at how the room is sparsely furnished with only a bed and a few books. He starts to question why he took such a long trip when what he sees doesn't match his expectation of someone so wise and well known. After engaging in some polite conversation with the Rabbi, the man cannot ignore his feelings anymore. He asks, "Rabbi, where are all your things?" After a moment of silence the Rabbi asks in return, "Well, where are yours?" The man answers by saying, "I am just passing through." The Rabbi then answers him by saying, "So am I, so am I."

The sooner we accept the realization that we will not lead forever, the sooner we can get to accomplishing the most important task before us.

We may not have realized this at the time we stepped or were called into leadership, but to have the most, long lasting success we must understand it is about serving and focusing on helping others replace us.

We must support, engage, and empower teachers because we want to ultimately create and build up more leaders. Think about the leaders who helped you achieve your current place. Picture the leaders you have helped get to theirs. It's true that we are all just passing through. The question is, what will we have created that is left behind? What will be our lasting impact? Our legacy?

The toughest journeys are those that do not follow a straight path. But it is on that weaving path where we learn; learn how to fail, and how to turn those failures into successes. It is on those weaving paths that we are building our legacy. And that's what makes the journey so much more important than the destination. I wish you, reader, good luck in this journey. It's incredibly difficult, but incredibly worth it. And isn't that why we're here?

ENDNOTES

[41] I first heard this story on Daniel Bauer's School Leadership Series podcast episode S3 E283 titled Just Passing Through. He found it in the book A Path With Heart by Jack Cornfield.

ABOUT THE AUTHOR

Chris Dr. Chris Jones has been an educator in Massachusetts for 22 years. His experience in the classroom ranged from 8th - 11th grade working in an urban setting. A portion of this was spent opening a high school division for an expanding charter school. He has just finished his 14th year as a building administrator. Chris is also the Vice President of the Massachusetts State Administrators Association (MSAA). True to his "why" of improving the educational experience for as many people as possible, he is currently the Principal of Whitman-Hanson Regional High School in Whitman, Massachusetts.

Chris is passionate about continuous improvement and the idea that success is not a destination, but a process. Chris is a teacher centered principal and his beliefs around the importance of a positive work environment, continuous growth, and a healthy family work-life integration can be seen in the presentations and workshops he has given for the Massachusetts School Administrators Association (MSAA), Massachusetts Computer Using Educators (MassCUE), Massachusetts Association of Supervision and Curriculum Development (MASCD), the Association of Supervision and Curriculum Development (ASCD), the National Association of Secondary School Principals (NASSP); and his participation in the Better Leaders Better Schools Mastermind group.

A finalist for the Massachusetts School Administrators Association's Principal of the Year award and named the 2022 Massachusetts School Counselors Associations (MASCA) Administrator of the Year, Chris is described by his past Superintendent as being *"...wholly invested in the success of the school...a creative problem-solver who is able to deliberate yet be decisive, be creative yet accountable...calm and clear-headed even under the most trying of times has built a strong collaborative and collegial school culture…he is a positive influence on teachers, teaching, and learning."*

Chris is active on Twitter, vlogs about continuous improvement on a weekly basis, and hosts his own podcast called SEEing to Lead as a way to amplify teachers' voices in an effort to improve education as a whole. His overarching goal is to positively model continuous improvement in all facets of life by being purposeful, acting with integrity, and building character.

Chris' education includes a BA from Bridgewater State University, an MA from Salem State University, and a Doctorate from Northeastern University. He currently resides in Southeastern Massachusetts with his wife, Mary (Bella) and two boys, Tommy and Scotty.

CODE BREAKER INC.

CONSULTING

To learn more about
DR. CHRISTOPHER JONES
or to book him for a visit to your school, district, or event, visit
www.codebreakeredu.com

INSPIRE · INNOVATE

LEAD · TEACH · LEARN

CODE BREAKER LEADERSHIP SERIES

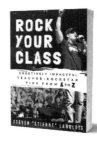

CODE BREAKER KID COLLECTION

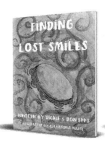

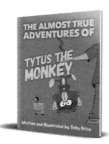

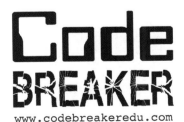

Made in the USA
Middletown, DE
11 May 2023

30427410R00073